訓練聽力 增加字彙

　　英語聽力是學習英語的重要一環，必須提早開始，長期訓練。而且要每月計畫的及復練習，絕不能只學聽單字認圖片，一定要聽句子，而且要逐漸拉長句子的內容，才能學習到英語的真諦。

　　本書是針對七、八、九年級學生的程度，循序漸進，逐步加強，期望能在 12 年國教的會考及特色招生考試中，一舉拿下聽力的滿分。本書的另一特色為在快樂學習中增加單字的記憶和使用能力，透過反覆的聽力訓練，不但大量增加字彙的累積，在不知不覺中也學會了說與寫的能力，可謂一舉數得，而且輕鬆易得。

　　為減輕學生的聽力障礙，本書將考題敘述的每個句子及答案，都精心譯為中文，以供學生參考。

　　在英語聽力測驗的出題「考點」中，我們歸納出下列幾個重點，請同學特別注意：

1. 隨時注意 7 個 W：who, when, what, where, which, why, how

　　也就是人、時、事、地、物、原因、狀態

2. 能夠與不能 (ability and inability)

　　常用字詞有：can, be able to, could, can't, couldn't, not be able to, neither

> 1)　A: How many languages can you speak?
> 　　B: I can/am able to speak three languages fluently.
> 　　翻譯：A：你能說幾種語言？
> 　　　　　B：我能流利的說三種語言。
>
> 2)　A: Has he bought a new house?
> 　　B: No. He's never been able to save money.
> 　　翻譯：A：他買新房子了嗎？
> 　　　　　B：不，他永遠沒有能力存錢。
>
> 3)　A: I couldn't do the homework. It was too difficult.
> 　　B: Neither could I.
> 　　翻譯：A：我不會做作業。太難了。
> 　　　　　B：我也不會。

3. 勸告與建議 (advice and suggestion)

　　常用字詞有：had better, I think, let's, OK, yes, good idea, sure, why not,

> 1)　A: I've got a headache today.
> 　　B: You'd better go to see the doctor./I think you should go to see the doctor.
> 　　翻譯：A：我今天頭痛。
> 　　　　　B：你最好去看醫生。我想你應該去看醫生。
>
> 2)　A: I've got a terrible stomachache.

B: You'd better not go on working.

A: OK./All right./Thank you for your advice.

翻譯：A：我的胃痛死了。

B：你最好不要上班。

C：好的/沒問題/謝謝你的勸告。

3) A: Let's go, shall we?

B: Yes, let's./I'm afraid it's too early.

翻譯：A：我們走吧，要不要？

B：好，走吧。/我怕太晚了。

4) A: What/How about going fishing now?

B: That's a good idea./That sounds interesting./Sure. Why not?

翻譯：A：現在去釣魚怎麼樣？

B：好主意。/聽起來很有趣。/當然，有何不可？

5) A: Let's go to the concert.

B: I don't feel like it. Why don't we go to the beach instead?

翻譯：A：我們去聽音樂會吧。

B：我不想去。我們為什麼不去海邊？

4. 同意與不同意 (agreement and disagreement)

常用字詞有：I think so. I hope so. I don't think so. I agree. I don't agree. So can I. Me too. Neither can I. I can't, either.

1) A: The book is interesting.

B: I think so, too.

翻譯：A：這本書很有趣。

B：我也這麼想。

2) A: Do you think people will be able to live on the moon in the future?

B: I hope so, but I don't think so.

翻譯：A：你認為人類將來能住到月球上嗎？

B：希望如此，但我不認為能夠。

3) A: This lesson is interesting, isn't it?

B: I don't think so./I'm afraid I can't agree with you./I'm afraid I don't quite agree with you./I'm afraid it isn't.

翻譯：A：這堂課很有趣，不是嗎？

B：我不這樣認為。恐怕我無法同意你。我恐怕不十分同意你。恐怕不是這樣。

4) A: I can swim well.

> B: So can I./Me too.
>
> 翻譯：A：我很會游泳。
>
> B：我也是。

5) A: I can't play the guitar.

B: Neither can I./I can't, either.

翻譯：A：我不會彈吉他。

B：我也不會。

5. 道歉（Apology）

常用字詞有：Sorry. I'm sorry about ....

> A: Sorry./I'm terribly sorry about that.
>
> B: That's all right./Never mind./Don't worry.
>
> 翻譯：A：抱歉。關於那件事我非常抱歉。
>
> B：沒關係。不要放在心上。不要擔心。

6. 讚賞（Appreciation）

常用字詞有：That's a good idea. That sounds interesting. Fantastic! Amazing! Well done！That's wonderful.

1) A: I've got the first prize.

B: Well done！/You deserved to win./That's wonderful news.

翻譯：A：我得第一名。

B：真棒。你實至名歸。真是個棒消息。

2) A: We had a surprise birthday party on Saturday afternoon.

B: That was a super afternoon.

翻譯：A：星期六下午的生日聚會令人驚喜。

B：那是個超棒的下午。

3) A: He broke the world record for the two mile run.

B: Fantastic!/Amazing!

翻譯：A：他在兩英哩賽跑打破世界紀錄。

B：了不起。又驚又喜。

7. 肯定與不肯定（certainty and uncertainty）

常用字詞有：sure, not sure, perhaps, maybe, possible, possibly,

1) A: Are you sure?

B: Yes, I am./No, I'm not.

翻譯：A：你確定嗎？

B：是的，我確定。不，我不確定。

2) A: When will Mary go to school?

B: Perhaps/Maybe she'll go at eight.

翻譯：A：Mary 何時上學？

B：或許 8 歲。

3) A: His ambition is to be an architect.

B: He'll possibly go to university after he leaves school.

翻譯：A：他的願望是當建築師。

B：他離開學校後可能要念大學。

8. 比較 (Comparison)

常用字詞有：as...as..., not so... as..., more... than..., less...than...,

1) A: How tall is Sue?

B: 1.6 meters. She's not so tall as Jane.

A: What about Mary?

B: She's as tall as Sue.

翻譯：A：Sue 身高多少。

B：160 公分。她不像 Jane 那麼高。

A：那 Mary 呢？

B：她跟 Sue 一樣高。

2) A: Which is more important, electricity or water?

B: It's hard to say.

翻譯：A：哪個比較重要，水還是電？

B：很難說。

9. 關心 (Concern)

常用字詞有：Is anything wrong? What's the matter? What's wrong with ....?
What's the matter with ....? How's ......?

1) A: What's wrong with you?/What's the matter with you?

B: I've got a cold.

翻譯：A：你怎麼了？

B：我感冒了。

2) A: How's your mother?

B: She's worse than yesterday.

A: I'm sorry to hear that. Don't worry too much. She'll get better soon.

翻譯：A：令堂狀況如何。

B：她比昨天更糟了。

> A：我聽了很遺憾。不用太擔心。她很快就會好一些。

4)　A: What's the matter?
　　B: I can't find my car key.
　　翻譯：A：發生甚麼事？
　　　　　B：我找不到汽車鑰匙。

10. 詢問 (Inquiries)

常用字詞有：How, when, where, who, why, what

1)　A: Excuse me, how can I get to the railway station?
　　B: Take a No. 41 bus.
　　翻譯：A：對不起，要如何到火車站去？
　　　　　B：搭 41 號公車。

2)　A: Excuse me. When does the next train leave for Kaohsuing?
　　B: 10 a.m.
　　翻譯：A：對不起。去高雄的下一班火車是甚麼時候？
　　　　　B：上午十點。

3)　A: What's the weather like today?
　　B: It'll rain this afternoon.
　　翻譯：A：今天天氣如何？
　　　　　B：下午會下雨。

4)　A: How far is your home from the school?
　　B: Five minutes by bike.
　　翻譯：A：你家距離學校有多遠？
　　　　　B：騎單車 5 分鐘。

11. 意向 (Intentions)

常用字詞有：I'd like …, Would you like to…? What do you want …?

1)　A: What do you want to be in the future?
　　B: I want to be a businessman.
　　翻譯：A：你將來想當甚麼？
　　　　　B：我想當生意人。

2)　A: Would you like to work at the South Pole in the future?
　　B: Yes, we'd love to.
　　翻譯：A：你將來喜歡在南極工作嗎？
　　　　　B：是的，我會喜歡。

3)　A: I'd like fried eggs with peas and pork, too.
　　B: OK.

翻譯：A：我想要豆子、豬肉炒蛋。
B：沒問題。

12. 喜歡、不喜歡/偏愛 (Likes, dislikes and preferences)

常用字詞有：like, dislike, prefer, enjoy

1) A: Which kind of apples do you prefer, red ones or green ones?
   B: Green ones.
   翻譯：A：你比較喜歡哪一種蘋果，紅的還是綠的？
   B：綠的。

2) A: Do you enjoy music or dance?
   B: I enjoy music.
   翻譯：A：你喜歡音樂還是跳舞？
   B：我喜歡音樂。

3) A: How did you like the play?
   B: It was wonderful.
   翻譯：A：這齣戲你覺得如何？
   B：很棒。

13. 提供 (Offers)

常用字詞有：Can I ....? Let me .... What can I ...? Would you like ...?

1) A: Can I help you?
   B: Yes, please.
   翻譯：A：可以幫你忙嗎？
   B：是的，謝謝。

2) A: Let me help you.
   B: Thanks.
   翻譯：A：我來幫你忙。
   B：謝謝。

3) A: Would you like a drink?
   B: That's very kind of you.
   翻譯：A：要來杯飲料嗎？
   B：你真好意。

4) A: Shall I get a trolley for you?
   B: No, thanks.
   翻譯：A：要我拿輛手推車給你嗎？
   B：不用，謝謝。

十二年國教特色招生及會考

全新英語聽力測驗

〔八年級／高階版（上）〕

目　次

全新英語聽力測驗試題
Unit 1

I、Listen and choose the right picture.（根據你所聽到的內容,選出相應的圖片。）
（6分）

A　　　　　B　　　　　C

D　　　　　E　　　　　F　　　　　G

1. _____　　2. _____　　3. _____

4. _____　　5. _____　　6. _____

II、Listen and choose the best response to the sentence you hear.（根據你所聽到的句子,選出最恰當的應答句。）（6分）

( ) 7.　(A)So do I.　　　　　　(B)So could I.
　　　　(C)Neither do I.　　　　(D)Neither could I.

( ) 8.　(A)About 10 minutes.　　(B)In 10 minutes.
　　　　(C)10-minute walk.　　　(D)For 10 minutes.

( ) 9.　(A)You'd better watch more TV.
　　　　(B)You'd better sleep late.
　　　　(C)You'd better sleep earlier.
　　　　(D)You'd better not go to see the doctor.

( ) 10. (A)That's a good idea. (B)That's right.
　　　　(C)That's all right. (D)Of course not.

( ) 11. (A)I hope so. (B)I hope not.
　　　　(C)I agree with you. (D)I don't like.

( ) 12. (A)At two o'clock. (B)For one hour.
　　　　(C)In two hours later. (D)Two hours.

Ⅲ、Listen to the dialogue and choose the best answer to the question you hear.
（根據你所聽到的對話和問題,選出最恰當的答案。）（6分）

( ) 13. (A)In the bookstore. (B)In the reading room.
　　　　(C)In the physics lab. (D)In the computer room.

( ) 14. (A)Because of the weather. (B)Because of his hobby.
　　　　(C)Because of his job. (D)Because of his age.

( ) 15. (A)In the classroom. (B)In the library.
　　　　(C)In the hospital. (D)In the dining room.

( ) 16. (A)Mary. (B)Peter.
　　　　(C)Tom. (D)John.

( ) 17. (A)At ten o'clock. (B)Before ten o'clock.
　　　　(C)Before twelve o'clock. (D)At about twelve o'clock.

( ) 18. (A)A secretary. (B)A waitress.
　　　　(C)A librarian. (D)A shop assistant.

Ⅳ、Listen to the dialogue and decide whether the following statements are True (T) or False (F). （判斷下列句子內容是否符合你所聽到的對話內容,符合的用"T"表示,不符合的用"F"表示。）（6分）

( ) 19. London is the largest city in the world.

( ) 20. London is very large, so it is difficult to see something interesting in the city centre.

( ) 21. Mandy liked the London buses because they went very fast.

( ) 22. Mandy saw David Beckham in the museum.

( ) 23. It was raining when Mandy was on the River Thames.

(　) 24.　Mandy has brought some photos that she took in China Town with her.

25.　Mary was often ill so she wanted to be _____. But she didn't know what to do.

26.　Miss Black told Mary that she must look after herself and then do something _____ for her health.

27.　Mary should do morning _____ and play sports.

28.　Mary must eat fruit and _____ and wash hands before meals.

29.　Mary shouldn't go to school without _____ in the morning.

30.　Mary shouldn't watch TV too , read in the sun or stay up late and so on.

全新英語聽力測驗試題
Unit 2

I、Listen and choose the right picture.（根據你所聽到的內容,選出相應的圖片。）
（6分）

A   B   C

D   E   F   G

1. _____   2. _____   3. _____

4. _____   5. _____   6. _____

II、Listen and choose the best response to the sentence you hear.（根據你所聽到的句子,選出最恰當的應答句。）（6分）

( ) 7.   (A)Yes, I will.   (B)No, I won't.
         (C)Yes, I won't.   (D)No, I will.

( ) 8.   (A)At three in the morning.   (B)In Shanghai.
         (C)With my parents.   (D)Taiwan.

( ) 9.   (A)Germany.   (B)China.
         (C)American.   (D)Australia.

( ) 10.   (A)So do I.   (B)Neither do I.
         (C)So have I.   (D)Neither haven't I.

( ) 11. (A)That's a good idea. (B)I'm afraid you are wrong.
(C)That's all right. (D)You are welcome.

( ) 12. (A)Here is it. (B)Here you are.
(C)It is here. (D)No, I don't.

Ⅲ、Listen to the dialogue and choose the best answer to the question you hear.
（根據你所聽到的對話和問題,選出最恰當的答案。）（6分）

( ) 13. (A)German. (B)American.
(C)English. (D)French.

( ) 14. (A)The teachers' office. (B)On the third floor.
(C)The library. (D)The lab.

( ) 15. (A)This Saturday. (B)This Sunday morning.
(C)At the airport. (D)At home.

( ) 16. (A)45. (B)15.
(C)30. (D)35.

( ) 17. (A)At a hotel. (B)At a clinic.
(C)In a supermarket. (D)In a shopping mall.

( ) 18. (A)1. (B)2.
(C)3. (D)4.

Ⅳ、Listen to the dialogue and decide whether the following statements are True (T) or False (F). (判斷下列句子內容是否符合你所聽到的對話內容,符合的用"T"表示,不符合的用"F"表示。)（6分）

( ) 19. Danny is an Australian.

( ) 20. One of his favorite interests is playing the guitar.

( ) 21. His job is to draw plans of buildings.

( ) 22. Danny has to work over 8 hours every day.

( ) 23. He never takes work home.

( ) 24. We keep in touch with each other twice a month.

Ⅴ、Listen and fill in the blanks.（根據你所聽到的內容,用適當的單詞完成下面的句子。每空格限填一詞。）（6分）

25. The man was going to fly to _____.

26. The man wanted the flight on the date of _____.

27. The number of the flight was _____.

28. The flight was at Gate _____, New York City Airport.

29. The departure time of the flight was at _____.

30. The man paid _____ for the ticket.

全新英語聽力測驗試題
Unit 3

I、Listen and choose the right picture.（根據你所聽到的內容,選出相應的圖片。）
（6分）

A   B   C

D   E   F   G

1. _____   2. _____   3. _____
4. _____   5. _____   6. _____

II、Listen and choose the best response to the sentence you hear.（根據你所聽到的句子,選出最恰當的應答句。）（6分）

(   ) 7. (A)I am a secretary.

    (B)I take notes and go to meetings with my manager.

    (C)I am happy with the job because it's very interesting.

    (D)I work in an office.

(   ) 8. (A)By subway.   (B)In subway.

    (C)At nine every morning. (D)I like my job.

(   ) 9. (A)No, you can't.   (B)Yes, you shall.

    (C)No, thanks.   (D)I think so.

( ) 10. (A)He works hard.
         (B)He brings food and drinks to the customers.
         (C)He delivers letters and parcels.
         (D)He draws plans of buildings.

( ) 11. (A)Each.   (B)No, I don't like doctors.
         (C)A teacher.   (D)Yes, I do.

( ) 12. (A)Never mind.   (B)Not at all.
         (C)All right.   (D)That's right.

Ⅲ、Listen to the dialogue and choose the best answer to the question you hear.
（根據你所聽到的對話和問題,選出最恰當的答案。）（6分）

( ) 13. (A)In the bookstore.   (B)In a police station.
         (C)At a canteen.   (D)In a post office.

( ) 14. (A)By car.   (B)By underground.
         (C)By taxi.   (D)On foot.

( ) 15. (A)At 1:00.   (B)At 1:30.
         (C)At 2:00.   (D)At 2:30.

( ) 16. (A)A teacher.   (B)An ambulance worker.
         (C)An office worker.   (D)An architect.

( ) 17. (A)He lives near the school.   (B)He lives far away from the school.
         (C)Yes, he does.   (D)No, he doesn't.

( ) 18. (A)25.   (B)30.
         (C)35.   (D)20.

Ⅳ、Listen to the dialogue and decide whether the following statements are True (T) or False (F). （判斷下列句子內容是否符合你所聽到的對話內容,符合的用"T"表示,不符合的用"F"表示。）（6分）

( ) 19. The man who went to the sea for his summer holidays was rich.

( ) 20. He asked his housekeeper to post him all the letters when he was not at home.

( ) 21. The housekeeper did not promise to post all the letters.

( ) 22. The man took the key to the letter box with him when he left home.

( ) 23. The man did not receive the letters until the next month.

( ) 24. When the man returned home, he was unhappy to speak to his housekeeper.

V、Listen and fill in the blanks.（根據你所聽到的內容,用適當的單詞完成下面的句子。每空格限填一詞。）（6分）

25. Jenny always wanted to be a _____.

26. Music was the most _____ thing in her life, but she has a terrible voice.

27. She _____ lessons for many years.

28. Her voice didn't become _____. In fact, it just got louder.

29. The teacher was very _____ about what to say after the concert.

30. She knew it _____ be a bad one.

全新英語聽力測驗試題
Unit 4

I、Listen and choose the right picture.（根據你所聽到的內容,選出相應的圖片。）
（6分）

A   B   C

D   E   F   G

1. _____   2. _____   3. _____

4. _____   5. _____   6. _____

II、Listen and choose the best response to the sentence you hear.（根據你所聽到的句子,選出最恰當的應答句。）（6分）

( ) 7.   (A)Good idea.   (B)No, I can't.
            (C)It's sunny.   (D)It's good for you.

( ) 8.   (A)Two months ago.   (B)For two months.
            (C)Since two months.   (D)In two months.

( ) 9.   (A)He is thirty years old.   (B)He is tall and thin.
            (C)He works hard.   (D)He is a police officer.

( ) 10.   (A)Thank you.   (B)No, I didn't.
             (C)Don't say so.   (D)I am not good.

( ) 11. (A)You are welcome. (B)With pleasure.
       (C)Of course not. (D)I agree.

( ) 12. (A)I'm a student. (B)I am reading a newspaper.
       (C)I have a bad headache. (D)I have been to the U.S.A. before.

Ⅲ、Listen to the dialogue and choose the best answer to the question you hear. （根據你所聽到的對話和問題,選出最恰當的答案。）（6分）

( ) 13. (A)4. (B)5. (C)6. (D)7.

( ) 14. (A)In the city center. (B)In the suburbs.
       (C)Both. (D)Neither.

( ) 15. (A)Near the shelf. (B)Next to the clock.
       (C)By the window. (D)On the sofa.

( ) 16. (A)He did his homework. (B)He watered flowers.
       (C)He cleaned the car with his father. (D)He watched TV.

( ) 17. (A)At a toy shop. (B)At a cloth shop.
       (C)At a CD shop. (D)At a furniture shop.

( ) 18. (A)Her father. (B)Her mother.
       (C)Her friend. (D)Her parents.

Ⅳ、Listen to the dialogue and decide whether the following statements are True (T) or False (F). （判斷下列句子內容是否符合你所聽到的對話內容,符合的用"T"表示,不符合的用"F"表示。）（6分）

( ) 19. Tom is a twelve-year-old boy.

( ) 20. Tom doesn't like any ball games.

( ) 21. Although Tom likes helping others, he is not careful.

( ) 22. Tom started a fire in his bedroom after his father left.

( ) 23. The firemen couldn't come because there was no fire engine.

( ) 24. What the fireman wanted to know was Tom's address.

Ⅴ、Listen and fill in the blanks. （根據你所聽到的內容,用適當的單詞完成下面的句子。每空格限填一詞。）（6分）

25. David is from _____.

26. He wants to live in the city center, because it's more _____.

27. Sunny Bay Agency has a flat with a sitting room, a _____ room, three bedrooms and two bathrooms.

28. The flat is about four _____ walk to the People's Square.

29. David should pay _____ yuan per month.

30. The agent's telephone number is _____.

全新英語聽力測驗試題
Unit 5

I、Listen and choose the right picture.（根據你所聽到的內容,選出相應的圖片。）
（6分）

A　　　　　　B　　　　　　C

D　　　　　　E　　　　　　F　　　　　　G

1. _____　　2. _____　　3. _____

4. _____　　5. _____　　6. _____

I、Listen and choose the best response to the sentence you hear.（根據你所聽到的句子,選出最恰當的應答句。）（6分）

(　) 7.　(A)A direction sign.　　　　(B)An information sign.
　　　　(C)An instruction sign.　　　(D)A warning sign.

(　) 8.　(A)Sorry, you mustn't.　　　(B)Yes, you may.
　　　　(C)There are flowers in the park.　(D)Flowers are nice.

(　) 9.　(A)I will take your advice.　　(B)That's good.
　　　　(C)You should study harder.　(D)I think so.

(　) 10.　(A)Thank you.　　　　　　(B)Don't say so.
　　　　(C)No, I don't.　　　　　　(D)That's all right.

( ) 11.　(A)Good idea.　　　　　　　　　(B)I think so, too.
　　　　　(C)Yes, I will.　　　　　　　　　(D)I'm glad.
( ) 12.　(A)For at least one hour.　　　　(B)In one hour.
　　　　　(C)At one o'clock.　　　　　　　(D)By one hour.

Ⅲ、Listen to the dialogue and choose the best answer to the question you hear.
（根據你所聽到的對話和問題,選出最恰當的答案。）（6分）

( ) 13.　(A)Yes, he can.　　　　　　　　(B)No, he can't.
　　　　　(C)Yes, he does.　　　　　　　(D)No, he doesn't.
( ) 14.　(A)At home.　　　　　　　　　(B)In the hospital.
　　　　　(C)At the zoo.　　　　　　　　(D)In the reading room.
( ) 15.　(A)An SPCA officer.　　　　　　(B)Homeless children.
　　　　　(C)Homeless animals.　　　　　(D)Three years ago.
( ) 16.　(A)10.　　　　　　　　　　　　(B)15.
　　　　　(C)20.　　　　　　　　　　　　(D)25.
( ) 17.　(A)A police officer.　　　　　　(B)To catch thieves.
　　　　　(C)To help others.　　　　　　(D)A doctor.
( ) 18.　(A)Wednesday.　　　　　　　　(B)Thursday.
　　　　　(C)Tuesday.　　　　　　　　　(D)Friday.

Ⅳ、Listen to the dialogue and decide whether the following statements are True (T) or False (F). （判斷下列句子內容是否符合你所聽到的對話內容,符合的用"T"表示,不符合的用"F"表示。）（6分）

( ) 19.　Mr and Mrs White went to the city centre on Saturday.

( ) 20.　When Mr and Mrs White returned home late, it was very dark in the room.

( ) 21.　Mr and Mrs White's bedroom is on the ground floor.

( ) 22.　On the way to the front door, they heard someone talking.

( ) 23.　Two boys broke into the house during the day time and stayed there.

( ) 24.　Mr White forgot to turn off the TV in the morning.

25. Good study habits are very _____.

26. When you have good study habits, you learn things _____.

27. When you study, don't think about _____ things at the same time.

28. If you do this, you will make _____ mistakes.

29. Every student should _____ good habits.

30. If your study habits are already good, try to make them _____.

全新英語聽力測驗試題
Unit 6

Ⅰ、Listen and choose the right picture.（根據你所聽到的內容,選出相應的圖片。）
（6分）

A   B   C

D   E   F   G

1. _____   2. _____   3. _____

4. _____   5. _____   6. _____

Ⅱ、Listen and choose the best response to the sentence you hear.（根據你所聽到的句子,選出最恰當的應答句。）（6分）

(　) 7.　(A)How do you do?　　　　　　(B)Good luck!
　　　　(C)Never mind.　　　　　　　(D)That's nothing.

(　) 8.　(A)So should I.　　　　　　　(B)Neither should I.
　　　　(C)I think so, too.　　　　　(D)I think not.

(　) 9.　(A)Yes, I could.　　　　　　(B)No, I couldn't.
　　　　(C)I haven't.　　　　　　　(D)Here you are.

(　) 10.　(A)Yes, you can.　　　　　　(B)No, you can't.
　　　　 (C)Sorry, I don't have time.　(D)Sure, go ahead.

( ) 11. (A)Yes, I am.

(B)I'm sorry, Miss Lin. I will come earlier next time.

(C)It doesn't matter.

(D)I think you are right.

( ) 12. (A)You'd better have more chocolate.

(B)You'd better eat more healthy food.

(C)You'd better watch more TV.

(D)You'd better do less exercise.

III、Listen to the dialogue and choose the best answer to the question you hear.
（根據你所聽到的對話和問題,選出最恰當的答案。）（6分）

( ) 13. (A)She's not busy.   (B)She is busy.

(C)She is ill in the hospital.   (D)She is talking.

( ) 14. (A)A lot of fruit and vegetables.   (B)Some ice cream.

(C)Some chocolate.   (D)All the above.

( ) 15. (A)22.   (B)24.

(C)38.   (D)48.

( ) 16. (A)Because she doesn't like table tennis.

(B)Because she will watch a football game.

(C)Because she will watch a basketball game.

(D)Because she will visit Nanpu Bridge.

( ) 17. (A)Tea.   (B)Coffee.

(C)Both.   (D)Neither.

( ) 18. (A)In the classroom.   (B)At Mark's home.

(C)On the phone.   (D)At the birthday party.

IV、Listen to the dialogue and decide whether the following statements are True (T) or False (F).（判斷下列句子內容是否符合你所聽到的對話內容,符合的用"T"表示,不符合的用"F"表示。）（6分）

( ) 19. Tea has a short history.

( ) 20. In China, people like to drink tea when they get together.

( ) 21. The Chinese only drink tea in the late afternoon.

( ) 22.　The Japanese have a special way of serving tea.

( ) 23.　The English like their tea with nothing else in it.

( ) 24.　The passage talks about different cultures of drinking tea in four countries.

V、Listen and fill in the blanks.（根據你所聽到的內容,用適當的單詞完成下面的句子。每空格限填一詞。）（6分）

25.　Jimmy's favourite food is _____ chicken, chocolate and ice cream.

26.　Jimmy's mother is worried about his health because he is fat and _____.

27.　Jimmy hates doing _____ but he likes watching TV at weekends.

28.　Last week, Jimmy was _____.

29.　Jimmy is not healthy because he has a bad _____.

30.　Jimmy thinks he will be _____ and healthier.

全新英語聽力測驗試題
Unit 7

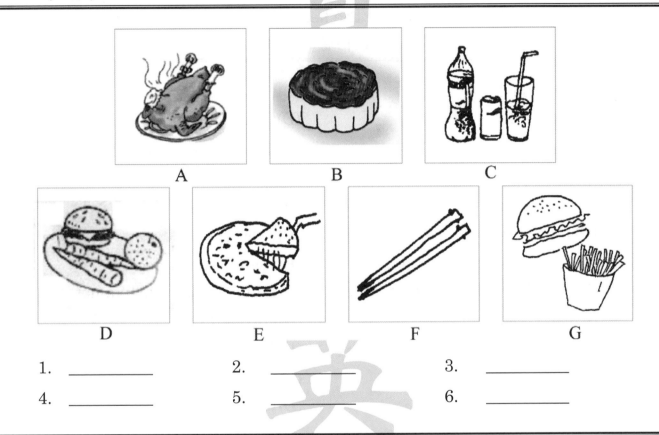

A B C

D E F G

1. _____   2. _____   3. _____

4. _____   5. _____   6. _____

Ⅱ、Listen and choose the best response to the sentence you hear.（根據你所聽到的句子,選出最恰當的應答句。）（6分）

( ) 7.　(A)That sounds great.　　　　　(B)I don't like any drinks.
　　　　(C)Let's have some drinks.　　　(D)Drinks are good for us.

( ) 8.　(A)It's November 1.　　　　　　(B)It's autumn.
　　　　(C)It's windy and cold.　　　　　(D)It's eight o'clock.

( ) 9.　(A)So is my brother.　　　　　　(B)Neither is my brother.
　　　　(C)So does my brother.　　　　　(D)Neither does my brother.

( ) 10.　(A)Hot dogs.　　　　　　　　　(B)Raisin Scones.
　　　　(C)Sushi.　　　　　　　　　　　(D)Rice dumplings.

(　)11.　(A)What a pity!　　　　　　　　(B)That's a great idea.

(C)What is a food festival?　　　(D)We hold it at school.

(　)12.　(A)I don't know.

(B)The police station is over there.

(C)Walk for two blocks and then turn right.

(D)The police station isn't far.

III、Listen to the dialogue and choose the best answer to the question you hear.
（根據你所聽到的對話和問題,選出最恰當的答案。）（6分）

(　)13.　(A)On June 13.　　　　　(B)On July 30.

(C)On June 30.　　　　　(D)On July 13.

(　)14.　(A)The Spring Festival.　　　(B)Mid-autumn Festival.

(C)Lantern Festival.　　　　(D)Dragon Boat Festival.

(　)15.　(A)Once a day.　　　　　(B)Once a week.

(C)Twice a day.　　　　　(D)Twice a week.

(　)16.　(A)John doesn't like hot dogs.　　(B)John likes hot dogs.

(C)The girl will give John a puppy.　(D)Eddie will give John a hot dog.

(　)17.　(A)Forty-two.　　　　　(B)Forty-six.

(C)Sixty-four.　　　　　(D)Thirty-one.

(　)18.　(A)Spring.　　　　　　(B)Summer.

(C)Autumn.　　　　　　(D)Winter.

IV、Listen to the dialogue and decide whether the following statements are True (T) or False (F). （判斷下列句子內容是否符合你所聽到的對話內容,符合的用"T"表示,不符合的用"F"表示。）（6分）

(　)19.　Today is Thanksgiving Day.

(　)20.　Jenny and her father went to her grandparents' home in the evening.

(　)21.　Jenny's grandmother cooked a turkey for them.

(　)22.　Jenny's grandmother made some apple pies.

(　)23.　Tom was playing with his toy horse when Jenny saw him.

(　)24.　After the meal, Jenny and her father still stayed there.

V、Listen and fill in the blanks.（根據你所聽到的內容,用適當的單詞完成下面的句子。每空格限填一詞。）（6分）

25. Japanese food is getting more and more _____.

26. The most _____ Japanese food is sushi, which you can buy in the supermarkets all around the world.

27. It's _____ to eat in the restaurants.

28. You can save a lot of money by _____ it yourself. And it's easy. There are lots of different ways of making sushi. Here is one way.

29. Put some _____, salt and vinegar in a cup.

30. Cut the salmon into, then press the salmon on top of the rice balls _____.

全新英語聽力測驗試題
Unit 8

Ⅰ、Listen and choose the right picture.（根據你所聽到的內容,選出相應的圖片。）（6分）

A   B   C

D   E   F   G

1. _____   2. _____   3. _____

4. _____   5. _____   6. _____

Ⅱ、Listen and choose the best response to the sentence you hear.（根據你所聽到的句子,選出最恰當的應答句。）（6分）

(　) 7.　(A)Yes, I do.　　　　　　　　　　(B)All right.
　　　　　(C)I'd like a cup of coffee.　　　(D)No, you needn't.

(　) 8.　(A)By foot.　　　　　　　　　　　(B)On foot.
　　　　　(C)By my father's car.　　　　　(D)On car.

(　) 9.　(A)You too.　　　　　　　　　　　(B)Thank you.
　　　　　(C)Nice to meet you, too.　　　　(D)Hello.

(　) 10.　(A)Thanks.　　　　　　　　　　　(B)No, it isn't.
　　　　　(C)Yes, I do.　　　　　　　　　　(D)No problem.

( ) 11.　(A)Each.　　　　　　　　　　(B)No, they aren't.

　　　　　(C)It's hard to say.　　　　　(D)Yes, they are.

( ) 12.　(A)He will be good.　　　　　(B)It's OK.

　　　　　(C)I'm sorry to hear that.　　(D)That's great!

Ⅲ、**Listen to the dialogue and choose the best answer to the question you hear.** （根據你所聽到的對話和問題,選出最恰當的答案。）（6分）

( ) 13.　(A)Hangzhou.　　　　　　　　(B)Shanghai.

　　　　　(C)Beijing.　　　　　　　　　(D)Guangzhou.

( ) 14.　(A)In a bank.　　　　　　　　(B)At a restaurant.

　　　　　(C)In an office.　　　　　　　(D)At the airport.

( ) 15.　(A)They are not delicious.　　(B)He is hungry.

　　　　　(C)He is full.　　　　　　　　(D)He doesn't like mooncakes.

( ) 16.　(A)Two days later.　　　　　　(B)Tomorrow.

　　　　　(C)Wednesday.　　　　　　　(D)Monday.

( ) 17.　(A)Do some revision.　　　　　(B)Have a good rest.

　　　　　(C)Go to bed late.　　　　　　(D)Do well in English.

( ) 18.　(A)No, she isn't.　　　　　　　(B)No, she is.

　　　　　(C)Yes, she is.　　　　　　　　(D)Yes, she isn't.

Ⅳ、**Listen to the dialogue and decide whether the following statements are True (T) or False (F).** （判斷下列句子內容是否符合你所聽到的對話內容,符合的用"T"表示,不符合的用"F"表示。）（6分）

( ) 19.　New Zealand is in South America.

( ) 20.　The old story in New Zealand says the God's parents created the world we live in.

( ) 21.　The theme of the New Zealand Pavilion is "Better city, better life".

( ) 22.　The pavilion has an area of 2,000 square meters.

( ) 23.　There are four parts in the New Zealand Pavilion.

( ) 24.　When people entered the pavilion, they could experience a day _____ in a New Zealand city.

25. Usually, I couldn't give an _____ when people ask me the question: when is the best time to visit Shanghai?

26. _____ may be the best time to visit Shanghai.

27. There are many _____ during the Shanghai Travel _____.

28. There are also many other _____ events during the three weeks in Shanghai.

29. I believe that _____ of the beauty of Shanghai is its lights.

全新英語聽力測驗試題
Unit 9

I、Listen and choose the right picture.（根據你所聽到的內容,選出相應的圖片。）（6分）

A   B   C

D   E   F   G

1. _____   2. _____   3. _____

4. _____   5. _____   6. _____

II、Listen and choose the best response to the sentence you hear.（根據你所聽到的句子,選出最恰當的應答句。）（6分）

( ) 7.   (A)The Adventures of Tom Sawyer.   (B)The Snow White.
    (C)The Swan Lake.   (D)The Happy Clown.

( ) 8.   (A)For two and a half hours.   (B)In two and a half hours.
    (C)The film is about love.   (D)What is the film about?

( ) 9.   (A)So do I.   (B)Neither do I.
    (C)So would I.   (D)Neither would I.

( ) 10.   (A)We must keep our bedroom clean.   (B)We must walk on the zebra lines.
     (C)We mustn't eat or drink here.   (D)We must obey the traffic rules.

( ) 11.　(A)Yes, I will.　　　　　　　　(B)It isn't late.
　　　　(C)Take care on your way home.　(D)With pleasure.

( ) 12.　(A)Never mind.　　　　　　　　(B)It doesn't matter.
　　　　(C)Thanks. It's kind of you.　　(D)Yes, I'd love to.

Ⅲ、Listen to the dialogue and choose the best answer to the question you hear.
　（根據你所聽到的對話和問題,選出最恰當的答案。）（6分）

( ) 13.　(A)In a shoe shop.　　　(B)At a supermarket.
　　　　(C)In a hotel.　　　　　(D)In a glass factory.

( ) 14.　(A)Operate the computer.　(B)Show Tom.
　　　　(C)Help Jim.　　　　　　(D)Look for the computer.

( ) 15.　(A)At 9:30.　　　　(B)At 10.
　　　　(C)At 10:30.　　　(D)At 11.

( ) 16.　(A)In a car.　　　(B)At the crossing.
　　　　(C)On a bus.　　　(D)At home.

( ) 17.　(A)On the 1st floor.　(B)On the 2nd floor.
　　　　(C)On the 5th floor.　(D)On the 6th floor.

( ) 18.　(A)Cartoons.　　　(B)Love stories.
　　　　(C)Adventures.　　(D)Horror films.

Ⅳ、Listen to the dialogue and decide whether the following statements are True (T) or False (F).（判斷下列句子內容是否符合你所聽到的對話內容,符合的用"T"表示,不符合的用"F"表示。）（6分）

( ) 19.　Movies are also called moving pictures.

( ) 20.　The boy's father sold pictures.

( ) 21.　The boy had to move fifty boxes of pictures from one room into another.

( ) 22.　His friend was very pleased to help the boy move pictures.

( ) 23.　At last, they saw an interesting film.

( ) 24.　In fact, the boy's friend liked watching films.

25. I saw a film called After Shocks in Shanghai Movie _____ at 6:30 p.m. last week.

26. The film tells a story about a _____ earthquake happened in Tangshan in 1976.

27. The film talks about human love and asks us to _____ our lives every day.

28. The film lasted for more than _____ hours.

29. I was _____ to tears.

30. When I went out of the cinema, it was nearly _____ p.m.

全新英語聽力測驗試題
Unit 10

I、Listen and choose the right picture.（根據你所聽到的內容,選出相應的圖片。）（6分）

A B C

D E F G

1. _____ 2. _____ 3. _____

4. _____ 5. _____ 6. _____

II、Listen and choose the best response to the sentence you hear.（根據你所聽到的句子,選出最恰當的應答句。）（6分）

( ) 7. (A)Shirts. (B)Sports shoes.
        (C)Size medium. (D)Clothes.

( ) 8. (A)No, you can't. (B)The jeans are over there.
        (C)Sure. (D)I don't like the color.

( ) 9. (A)It doesn't matter. (B)No, you don't.
        (C)Yes, you do. (D)Don't bother me.

( ) 10. (A)What's the matter? (B)Sure. What time?
         (C)Yes, I do. (D)The ball will be at my place.

( ) 11.　(A)So do I.　　　　　　　　(B)So I do.

　　　　(C)Neither do I.　　　　　　(D)Neither I do.

( ) 12.　(A)Three hours.　　　　　　(B)In three hours.

　　　　(C)At three o'clock.　　　　(D)Since three hours.

Ⅲ、Listen to the dialogue and choose the best answer to the question you hear.
（根據你所聽到的對話和問題,選出最恰當的答案。）（6分）

( ) 13.　(A)He doesn't like the style.　　(B)He doesn't like the colour.

　　　　(C)The size is too big.　　　　(D)The size is too small.

( ) 14.　(A)4 yuan.　　　　　　　　(B)8 yuan.

　　　　(C)12 yuan.　　　　　　　(D)14 yuan.

( ) 15.　(A)A hat.　　　　　　　　(B)Bracelet.

　　　　(C)Earrings.　　　　　　　(D)Glasses.

( ) 16.　(A)For three years.　　　　(B)For four years.

　　　　(C)For five years.　　　　　(D)For six years.

( ) 17.　(A)10 dollars.　　　　　　(B)15 dollars.

　　　　(C)20 dollars.　　　　　　(D)25 dollars.

( ) 18.　(A)At a clothes shop.　　　　(B)In a restaurant.

　　　　(C)At an office.　　　　　　(D)In the fire station.

Ⅳ、Listen to the dialogue and decide whether the following statements are True (T) or False (F). （判斷下列句子內容是否符合你所聽到的對話內容,符合的用"T"表示,不符合的用"F"表示。）（6分）

( ) 19.　Lin Miaoke became famous after the 2008 Beijing Olympic Games.

( ) 20.　Lin Miaoke sang the song "A Hymn to My motherland"　at the opening ceremony.

( ) 21.　She likes playing the piano and flute, but she can't dance.

( ) 22.　She was six years old when she appeared in the TV advertisement with Liu Xiang.

( ) 23.　The director Zhang Yimou chose her among all the children in Shanghai.

( ) 24.　Now we can see her photos on many newspapers and magazines.

V、Listen and fill in the blanks.（根據你所聽到的內容,用適當的單詞完成下面的句子。每空格限填一詞。）（6分）

25. The woman wants to buy a pair of _____ shoes.

26. The _____ pair is 200 dollars.

27. The white pair _____ the woman well.

28. The white pair is _____ dollars.

29. The woman likes the T-shirt with red _____.

30. The woman will pay _____ dollars for them.

全新英語聽力測驗試題
Unit 11

I、Listen and choose the right picture.（根據你所聽到的內容,選出相應的圖片。）
（6分）

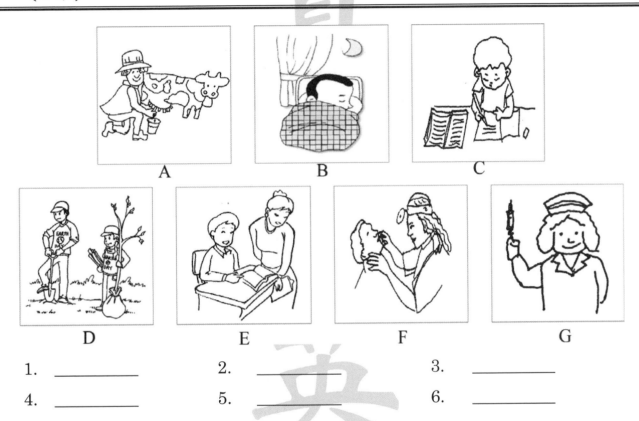

A   B   C

D   E   F   G

1. _____   2. _____   3. _____

4. _____   5. _____   6. _____

II、Listen and choose the best response to the sentence you hear.（根據你所聽到的句子,選出最恰當的應答句。）（6分）

( ) 7.   (A)To the library.   (B)This Sunday.
           (C)At 3 o'clock.   (D)Once a week.

( ) 8.   (A)I'm glad you like it.   (B)It's good.
           (C)Yes, it is.   (D)I'm sorry to hear that.

( ) 9.   (A)That's all right.   (B)You are welcome.
           (C)Thank you for your advice.   (D)No, I won't.

( ) 10.　(A)I have got a bad cold.

　　　　(B)I will go to the park tomorrow.

　　　　(C)I am doing my homework.

　　　　(D)There is something wrong with me.

( ) 11.　(A)So can I.　　　　　　　　　(B)Neither can I.

　　　　(C)So can't I.　　　　　　　　(D)Neither can't I.

( ) 12.　(A)Much better. Thank you.　　　(B)I'm better. Thanks.

　　　　(C)He's writing a report.　　　　(D)You are so kind.

Ⅲ、Listen to the dialogue and choose the best answer to the question you hear.
（根據你所聽到的對話和問題,選出最恰當的答案。）（6分）

( ) 13.　(A)At the cinema.　　　　　　　(B)On the school playground.

　　　　(C)At the clinic.　　　　　　　(D)In the hospital.

( ) 14.　(A)A teacher.　　　　　　　　(B)A reporter.

　　　　(C)A doctor.　　　　　　　　(D)A scientist.

( ) 15.　(A)At 6.　　　　　　　　　　(B)At 7.

　　　　(C)At 6:30.　　　　　　　　(D)At 7:30.

( ) 16.　(A)It will be rainy.　　　　　　(B)It will be cloudy.

　　　　(C)It will be snowy.　　　　　(D)It will be windy.

( ) 17.　(A)Lily.　　　　　　　　　　(B)Peter.

　　　　(C)Tom.　　　　　　　　　　(D)Jack.

( ) 18.　(A)Milk.　　　　　　　　　　(B)Bread.

　　　　(C)Pizza.　　　　　　　　　(D)Noodles.

Ⅳ、Listen to the dialogue and decide whether the following statements are True (T) or False (F).（判斷下列句子內容是否符合你所聽到的對話內容,符合的用"T"表示,不符合的用"F"表示。）（6分）

( ) 19.　Jimmy is good at all his subjects.

( ) 20.　Jimmy always does a lot of math problems.

( ) 21.　It takes Kitty about 40 minutes to get to school.

( ) 22.　Kitty takes a bus first and then she takes the underground.

( ) 23.　Tom couldn't answer his brother's question.

( ) 24.　Tom is a model student now.

V、Listen and fill in the blanks.（根據你所聽到的內容,用適當的單詞完成下面的句子。每空格限填一詞。）（6分）

Dear Alice,

　　12 __25__ is my birthday. I'd like to __26__ you to my birthday party. The party will __27__ at 6 p.m. at my flat. Many of our friends are coming. We are going to have a __28__ in the garden. We are also going to sing karaoke. We'll watch __29__, too. I hope you will be __30__ that day. See you then.

Yours,
Jenny

全新英語聽力測驗試題
Unit 12

I、Listen and choose the right picture. (根據你所聽到的內容,選出相應的圖片。)
（6分）

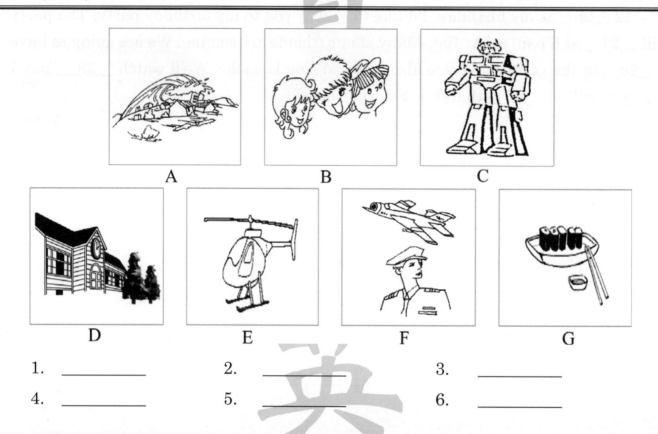

A   B   C

D   E   F   G

1. _____   2. _____   3. _____

4. _____   5. _____   6. _____

II、Listen and choose the best response to the sentence you hear. (根據你所聽到的句子,選出最恰當的應答句。)（6分）

(　　) 7.　(A)I think not.　　　　　　(B)I think so, too.
　　　　　(C)Yes, I do.　　　　　　　(D)So will we.

(　　) 8.　(A)How much are the tomatoes?　(B)OK. Ten yuan, please.
　　　　　(C)The tomatoes are fresh.　　(D)At the market.

(　　) 9.　(A)You are welcome.
　　　　　(B)Never mind. Take care next time.
　　　　　(C)All right.
　　　　　(D)Here you are.

( ) 10. (A)Would you like to come to my party?
(B)Come to my party.
(C)My party is great.
(D)You must come to my party.

( ) 11. (A)In the morning.   (B)In Japan.
(C)In April.   (D)It is Sunday.

( ) 12. (A)Yes, I can.   (B)No, I can't.
(C)With pleasure.   (D)Thank you.

Ⅲ、Listen to the dialogue and choose the best answer to the question you hear.
（根據你所聽到的對話和問題,選出最恰當的答案。）（6分）

( ) 13. (A)Action films.   (B)Funny films.
(C)Documentaries.   (D)Love stories.

( ) 14. (A)120 yuan.   (B)150 yuan.
(C)270 yuan.   (D)300 yuan.

( ) 15. (A)On foot.   (B)By bike.
(C)By bus.   (D)By taxi.

( ) 16. (A)Shanghai Zoo.   (B)Dongping National Forest Park.
(C)Changfeng Park.   (D)Nanjing Road.

( ) 17. (A)Spring.   (B)Summer.   (C)Autumn.   (D)Winter.

( ) 18. (A)Green.   (B)Yellow.   (C)Blue.   (D)Black.

Ⅳ、Listen to the dialogue and decide whether the following statements are True (T) or False (F). （判斷下列句子內容是否符合你所聽到的對話內容,符合的用"T"表示,不符合的用"F"表示。）（6分）

( ) 19. In the year 2015, there will be different kinds of materials for clothes.

( ) 20. The special clothes will easily get dirty.

( ) 21. Because of the special clothes, we will save water and money.

( ) 22. Children need to wear uniforms at school every day in 2050.

( ) 23. Children will stay at home and learn things by computer.

(　)24.　According to the writer, children will be able to design their favorite clothes.

V、Listen and fill in the blanks.（根據你所聽到的內容,用適當的單詞完成下面的句子。每空格限填一詞。）（6分）

1.　Tina looks _____.

2.　The _____ in some parts of the world will keep dropping.

3.　And there will be heavy snowstorm and floods _____.

4.　Although there is terrible air _____, Mike thinks we can solve the problem.

5.　Perhaps we can move to another _____ by spacecraft.

6.　Let's do something to _____ the earth from now on.

全新英語聽力測驗試題
Unit 13

A   B   C

D   E   F   G

1. _____   2. _____   3. _____

4. _____   5. _____   6. _____

Ⅱ、Listen and choose the best response to the sentence you hear.（根據你所聽到的句子,選出最恰當的應答句。）（6分）

( ) 7.   (A)So do mine.   (B)Neither do mine.
         (C)So is mine.   (D)Neither is mine.

( ) 8.   (A)Yes, I can.   (B)No, I can't.
         (C)I'm sorry to have bothered you.   (D)Yes, I could.

( ) 9.   (A)Yes, I am.   (B)Yes, he is.
         (C)Yes, speaking.   (D)I'm Mr Brown.

( ) 10. (A)What a pity!   (B)What fun!
         (C)I know.   (D)I don't think so.

( ) 11. (A)Certainly. (B)That's all right.
(C)That's right. (D)You're welcome.

( ) 12. (A)In a day. (B)Twice a day.
(C)At 7 o'clock. (D)For two times.

Ⅲ、Listen to the dialogue and choose the best answer to the question you hear.
（根據你所聽到的對話和問題,選出最恰當的答案。）（6分）

( ) 13. (A)At the weekend. (B)On weekdays.
(C)On Saturday. (D)On Sunday.

( ) 14. (A)6624594. (B)6627594.
(C)6627495. (D)6624495.

( ) 15. (A)They are looking at the photo. (B)They are visiting a kindergarten.
(C)They are talking to an aunt. (D)They are watching TV.

( ) 16. (A)A student. (B)A nurse.
(C)A teacher. (D)A doctor.

( ) 17. (A)10:45. (B)9:45.
(C)11:45. (D)8:45.

( ) 18. (A)To a post office. (B)To a food shop.
(C)To a library. (D)To a bank.

Ⅳ、Listen to the dialogue and decide whether the following statements are True (T) or False (F). (判斷下列句子內容是否符合你所聽到的對話內容,符合的用"T"表示,不符合的用"F"表示。)（6分）

( ) 19. Forests are important to us.

( ) 20. Trees only provide food for animals.

( ) 21. Animals will die quickly without trees.

( ) 22. Cans are made of clay.

( ) 23. Glass is made from sand on the beaches.

( ) 24. Everything we use in our daily life comes from trees and land.

25. The mudslide happened in early _____ in Gansu.

26. Many people were _____.

27. About _____ people died.

28. We had a _____ class just now.

29. We've decided to _____ some money for them.

30. The boy's father is an _____.

全新英語聽力測驗試題
Unit 14

Ⅰ、Listen and choose the right picture.（根據你所聽到的內容,選出相應的圖片。）
（6分）

1. _____   2. _____   3. _____
4. _____   5. _____   6. _____

Ⅱ、Listen and choose the best response to the sentence you hear.（根據你所聽到的句子,選出最恰當的應答句。）（6分）

( ) 7.　(A)I'm Jenny.　　　　　　　　(B)Yes, I am.
　　　　(C)Sorry, she isn't here.　　　　(D)Who are you?

( ) 8.　(A)We are friends.　　　　　　(B)We are fine. Thanks.
　　　　(C)We have been to Japan.　　(D)We will stay at home.

( ) 9.　(A)After three days.　　　　　　(B)At midnight.
　　　　(C)Three days later.　　　　　(D)Since three days.

( ) 10.　(A)I've lost my key rings.　　　(B)I'm 15 years old.
　　　　(C)I will buy a new shirt.　　　(D)I am right.

( ) 11. (A)To Beijing. (B)100 yuan.
(C)At five in the afternoon. (D)It's for sale.

( ) 12. (A)Bye bye. (B)Hello. Nice to meet you.
(C)What's your name? (D)Who's your friend?

Ⅲ、**Listen to the dialogue and choose the best answer to the question you hear.**
（根據你所聽到的對話和問題,選出最恰當的答案。）（6分）

( ) 13. (A)3:30. (B)3:40.
(C)3:50. (D)4:00.

( ) 14. (A)Snow. (B)Skating.
(C)Coldness. (D)Warm clothes.

( ) 15. (A)80 yuan. (B)100 yuan.
(C)60 yuan. (D)120 yuan.

( ) 16. (A)A shop assistant. (B)A book seller.
(C)A librarian. (D)A secretary.

( ) 17. (A)Rainy. (B)Stormy.
(C)Foggy. (D)Sunny.

( ) 18. (A)To eat mooncakes. (B)To set off firecrackers.
(C)To receive red packets. (D)To visit relatives.

Ⅳ、**Listen to the dialogue and decide whether the following statements are True (T) or False (F).** （判斷下列句子內容是否符合你所聽到的對話內容,符合的用"T"表示,不符合的用"F"表示。）（6分）

( ) 19. There are more than thirty million kinds of plants in the world.

( ) 20. People like decorating rooms with flowers and other plants.

( ) 21. People and animals only get food from plants.

( ) 22. Unlike animals, people can't live without plants.

( ) 23. People can make clothes out of cotton.

( ) 24. All medicines are made from plants.

V、Listen and fill in the blanks.（根據你所聽到的內容,用適當的單詞完成下面的句子。每空格限填一詞。）（6分）

25. Sports help to keep people healthy and make them live _____.

26. Sports change with the _____.

27. Sailing is _____ in warm weather.

28. _____ is good in winter.

29. People from different _____ may not be able to understand each other, but after a game on the sports field, they often become good friends.

30. One learns to fight hard, to win without pride and to _____ with grace.

全新英語聽力測驗試題
Final Test

I、Listen and choose the right picture.（根據你所聽到的內容,選出相應的圖片。）
（6分）

A   B   C

D   E   F   G

1. _____   2. _____   3. _____

4. _____   5. _____   6. _____

II、Listen and choose the best response to the sentence you hear.（根據你所聽到的句子,選出最恰當的應答句。）（6分）

(   ) 7.   (A)I'm fine.   (B)We get on well with each other.
           (C)He is clever.   (D)Yes, we do.

(   ) 8.   (A)She is good.   (B)She likes music.
           (C)She is tall and slim.   (D)She is reading books.

(   ) 9.   (A)So have I.   (B)Neither haven't I.
           (C)So haven't I.   (D)Neither have I.

(   ) 10.   (A)I don't think so .   (B)OK, let's.
           (C)That's all right.   (D)That's right.

( ) 11.　(A)Thank you.　　　　　　　　　　(B)I hope not.

　　　　(C)It's good.　　　　　　　　　　　(D)Yes, I have.

( ) 12.　(A)Really? Congratulations!　　　　(B)Thanks.

　　　　(C)It's nothing.　　　　　　　　　　(D)Don't say so.

Ⅲ、Listen to the dialogue and choose the best answer to the question you hear.
（根據你所聽到的對話和問題,選出最恰當的答案。）（6分）

( ) 13.　(A)More display boards.

　　　　(B)More interesting clubs.

　　　　(C)More books and children's magazines in the library.

　　　　(D)Less homework.

( ) 14.　(A)2.5 yuan.　　　　　　　　　　　(B)3 yuan.

　　　　(C)5 yuan.　　　　　　　　　　　　(D)3.5 yuan.

( ) 15.　(A)In Grade 9.　　　　　　　　　　(B)In Grade 8.

　　　　(C)In Grade 7.　　　　　　　　　　(D)In Grade 6.

( ) 16.　(A)Linda.　　　　　　　　　　　　(B)Fred.

　　　　(C)Both.　　　　　　　　　　　　　(D)Neither.

( ) 17.　(A)6:30.　　　　　　　　　　　　　(B)6:25.

　　　　(C)6:35.　　　　　　　　　　　　　(D)6:20.

( ) 18.　(A)At a restaurant.　　　　　　　　(B)In an office.

　　　　(C)At the post office.　　　　　　　(D)At the police station.

Ⅳ、Listen to the dialogue and decide whether the following statements are True (T) or False (F).（判斷下列句子內容是否符合你所聽到的對話內容,符合的用"T"表示,不符合的用"F"表示。）（6分）

( ) 19.　The aeroplane was flying from London to Los Angeles.

( ) 20.　There are four engines on the plane.

( ) 21.　The aeroplane can't fly on only three engines.

( ) 22.　When the third engine stopped, one of the passengers went to see the captain.

( ) 23.　If the last engine stopped, all the passengers would die.

(　　) 24.　In the end, the aeroplane arrived in London two hours late.

25.　Shaking hands is a way to show a person is _____.

26.　The legal drinking age in Germany is _____.

27.　Take _____ if you are invited to a German's home.

28.　Knock before you _____ an office.

29.　_____ food and drinks for all the people if you have a _____ party.

全新英語聽力測驗原文及參考答案

Unit 1

I、Listen and choose the right picture.（根據你所聽到的內容,選出相應的圖片。）
（6分）

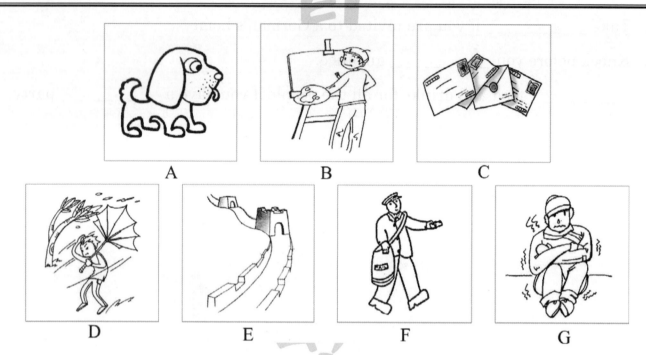

1. The wind is blowing so hard that the boy can't walk forwards easily.
   （風吹得太強了以至於男孩很難往前走。）

   答案：(D)

2. We are going to visit the Great Wall during our stay in Beijing.
   （我們待在北京的時候要去參觀萬里長城。）

   答案：(E)

3. What a lovely puppy! I hope to have one as my pet, too.
   （好可愛的小狗！我也希望有一隻當作我的寵物。）

   答案：(A)

4. I've just got some letters from my new pen friend.
   （我剛剛收到我新筆友的來信。）

   答案：(C)

5. Jack feels so cold now because he has had a cold.
    （Jack 現在覺得很冷，因為他已經感冒了。）
    答案：(G)

6. My brother's ambition is to be an artist, so he practices drawing every day.
    （我哥哥的志向是當藝術家，所以他每天練習作畫。）
    答案：(B)

Ⅱ、Listen and choose the best response to the sentence you hear.（根據你所聽到的句子,選出最恰當的應答句。）（6分）

7. I couldn't do the math problem. It's too difficult.（我不會做這道數學題。太難了。）
    (A)So do I.（我也做。）　　　　　(B)So could I.（我也會。）
    (C)Neither do I.（我也不做。）　　(D)Neither could I.（我也不會。）
    答案：(D)

8. How far is it from the subway station to your school?
    （從地鐵站去你的學校有多遠？）
    (A)About 10 minutes.（大約十分鐘。）(B)In 10 minutes.（十分鐘之內。）
    (C)10-minute walk.（十分鐘的路程。）(D)For 10 minutes.（要十分鐘。）
    答案：(C)

9. I've got a terrible headache.（我頭很痛。）
    (A)You'd better watch more TV.（你最好多看電視。）
    (B)You'd better sleep late.（你最好晚一點睡。）
    (C)You'd better sleep earlier.（你最好早一點睡。）
    (D)You'd better not go to see the doctor.（你最好不要去看醫生。）
    答案：(C)

10. Shall we go to see the film?（我們去看電影好嗎？）
    (A)That's a good idea.（好主意。）　　(B)That's right.（對。）
    (C)That's all right.（沒關係。）　　　(D)Of course not.（當然不好。）
    答案：(A)

11. Vegetables are good for us.（蔬菜對我們有益。）
    (A)I hope so.（我希望如此。）　　　(B)I hope not.（我不希望。）
    (C)I agree with you.（我同意。）　　(D)I don't like.（我不喜歡。）

答案：(C)

12. When will the meeting start?（會議甚麼時候開始？）

    (A)At two o'clock.（兩點。）   (B)For one hour.（要一個小時。）

    (C)In two hours later.（兩小時後。）   (D)Two hours.（兩小時。）

答案：(A)

Ⅲ、Listen to the dialogue and choose the best answer to the question you hear.
（根據你所聽到的對話和問題,選出最恰當的答案。）（6分）

---

13. W: What kind of books have you chosen, James?

    （W: James，你挑了哪種書？）

    M: Some books on computers. What about you?

    （M: 一些電腦書。妳呢？）

    W: I want to buy some physics books for my son. Where can I find them?

    （W: 我想幫我兒子買一些物理書。我在哪裡可以找到？）

    M: On the third floor.（M: 在三樓。）

    Q: Where does the dialogue probably take place?（Q: 這段對話大概在哪裡發生？）

    (A)In the bookstore.（在書店。）

    (B)In the reading room.（在閱覽室。）

    (C)In the physics lab.（在物理實驗室。）

    (D)In the computer room.（在電腦室。）

答案：(A)

14. W: Why does Jim get up so early?（W: 為什麼 Jim 起這麼早？）

    M: Because he works as a newspaper deliverer.

    （M: 因為他是送報員。）

    Q: Why does Jim get up early?（Q: 為什麼 Jim 起得早？）

    (A)Because of the weather.（因為天氣。）

    (B)Because of his hobby.（因為他的嗜好。）

    (C)Because of his job.（因為他的工作。）

    (D)Because of his age.（因為他的年齡。）

答案：(C)

15. W: Look, there's a sign on the wall. What does this sign mean?

    （W: 看，牆上有一個標示。這個標示是甚麼意思？）

M: It means we mustn't drink or eat here in the library.

（M: 它的意思是我們不能在圖書館內飲食。）

Q: Where are they speaking?（Q: 他們在哪裡談話？）

(A)In the classroom.（在教室。）   (B)In the library.（在圖書館。）

(C)In the hospital.（在醫院。）   (D)In the dining room.（在餐廳。）

答案：(B)

16. W: Who studies hardest, Mary, John or Peter?

（W: 誰最努力讀書，Mary、John 還是 Peter？）

M: Well... Mary studies harder than John, but not as hard as Peter.

（M: 嗯...Mary 比 John 努力，但是不像 Peter 那麼努力。）

Q: Who studies hardest?（Q: 誰最努力讀書？）

(A)Mary.   (B)Peter.   (C)Tom.   (D)John.

答案：(B)

17. W: What's the matter with you?（W: 你怎麼了？）

M: I have a headache.（M: 我頭痛。）

W: When did you go to bed last night?（W: 你昨晚幾點睡？）

M: I usually go to bed before ten o'clock. But yesterday I had much work to do and didn't go to bed until midnight.

（M: 我通常十點前就睡了。但是昨天我有太多工作要做，所以一直到半夜才睡。）

Q: When did the man go to bed last night?（Q: 那個男人昨天晚上幾點睡？）

(A)At ten o'clock.（十點。）

(B)Before ten o'clock.（十點之前。）

(C)Before twelve o'clock.（十二點之前。）

(D)At about twelve o'clock.（大約十二點。）

答案：(D)

18. W: Good morning, sir. Can I help you?（W: 先生，早安。我能為你服務嗎？）

M: Yes. I'd like a chicken roll, a green salad and some mushroom soup.

（M: 是的。我想要一個雞肉捲、沙拉、和蘑菇湯。）

W: Something to drink?（W: 要來點喝的嗎？）

M: No, thanks.（M: 不了，謝謝。）

W: A chicken roll, a green salad and some mushroom soup. OK, sir. The food will be ready soon.

（W: 一個雞肉捲、沙拉、和蘑菇湯。好的，先生。餐點馬上就準備好了。）

Q: What is the woman? (Q:那個女人是做甚麼的？)
(A)A secretary. (秘書。)　　　　　　　(B)A waitress. (服務生。)
(C)A librarian. (圖書管理員。)　　　　(D)A shop assistant. (店員。)
答案：(B)

IV、Listen to the dialogue and decide whether the following statements are True (T) or False (F). (判斷下列句子內容是否符合你所聽到的對話內容,符合的用"T"表示,不符合的用"F"表示。)（6分）

Mandy：Hi, Simon. It's wonderful to see you here again!

Mandy：嗨，Simon。真開心又在這裡看到你。

Simon：How was London, Mandy?

Simon：Mandy，倫敦怎麼樣？

Mandy：It was great! There is so much to see and so many things to do! I loved seeing all the different kinds of people there.

Mandy：好棒！有好多可看的，也有好多可做的。在那裡看到各式各樣的人，我愛死了。

Simon：What do you mean by "different kinds of people"？

Simon：「各式各樣的人」是甚麼意思？

Mandy：People from different places. It's fun just to look at all their faces.

Mandy：從各地來的人。光是看他們的臉就很有趣。

Simon：Is London a very big city?

Simon：倫敦是個非常大的城市嗎？

Mandy：Well, yes. It's the biggest city in Europe, and most of the interesting places are near the city centre.

Mandy：是。它是歐洲最大的城市，而且大部分有趣的地方都在市中心附近。

Simon：What did you like best about London?

Simon：妳最喜歡倫敦的甚麼？

Mandy：Well, I loved the buses. We travelled around the city on a double-decker bus every day. I always sat upstairs so that I could see better. We saw the Queen's Palace, though we didn't see the Queen. We also went to a wax museum. It had statues of all the most famous people in the world. I saw one of David Beckham. It looked like a real person. I even saw someone trying to ask a statue a question!

Mandy：我喜歡公車。我們每天搭雙層公車遊覽市區。我總是坐在上層，所以我可以看得更清楚。我們看到女王的皇宮，雖然我們沒看到女王。我們也去了蠟像博物館。那兒有世界上所有知名人士的蠟像。我看到貝克漢的蠟像。看起來好像真人。我甚至看到有人對著蠟像問問題！

Simon：Did you go on the river?

Simon：妳去河上遊覽了嗎？

Mandy：Yes. We sailed down the River Thames in a boat. It was raining, but still it was interesting to see all the famous old bridges. Oh, here's the waiter. Let's order our food, and then I'll show you my photos of China Town.

Mandy：去了。我們搭船在泰晤士河航行。那天正下著雨，但是看到所有知名的古老橋樑還是很有趣。喔，服務生來了。我們來點餐吧，然後我要給你看我在中國城拍的相片。

19. London is the largest city in the world. （倫敦是世界上最大的城市。）

答案：(F 錯)

20. London is very large, so it is difficult to see something interesting in the city centre. （倫敦非常大，所以在市中心很難看到有趣的事。）

答案：(F 錯)

21. Mandy liked the London buses because they went very fast.

（Many 喜歡倫敦公車因為它們開得非常快。）

答案：(F 錯)

22. Mandy saw David Beckham in the museum. （Mandy 在博物館看到貝克漢。）

答案：(F 錯)

23. It was raining when Mandy was on the River Thames.

（當 Mandy 在泰晤士河上的時候正在下雨。）

答案：(T 對)

24. Mandy has brought some photos that she took in China Town with her.

（Mandy 帶了她在中國城拍的相片。）

答案：(T 對)

V、Listen and fill in the blanks. （根據你所聽到的內容,用適當的單詞完成下面的句子。每空格限填一詞。）（6分）

Mary was not in good health. She was often ill. She wanted to be healthy but she didn't know what to do. One day, she asked Miss Black how to keep healthy. Miss Black told her, "First, you must look after yourself and then do something necessary for your health. For example, take a walk after supper, do morning exercises, play sports, eat fruit and vegetables, and wash your hands before meals. All of these things are good for your health."

Mary 的健康不大好。她常常生病。她想要健康但是不知道該怎麼做。有一天，她問 Black 小姐該如何保持健康。Black 小姐對她說：「首先，你必須照顧你自己，為你的健康做一些必要的事。例如：晚餐後散步、做晨間體操、做體育運動、吃水果和蔬菜、餐前洗手。以上所有的事都對你的健康有益。」

Miss Black went on, "Remember! Don't do anything bad for your health, like going to school without breakfast, keeping your fingernails long, watching TV too much, reading in the sun, staying up late and so on."

Black 小姐接著說：「要記住！不要做對健康有害的事，像是不吃早餐就去上學、留長指甲、看太多電視、在太陽底下看書、熬夜…等等。」

After that Mary always did as Miss Black told her. She is very healthy now.

在此之後，Mary 總是依照 Black 小姐告訴她的來做。她現在非常健康。

---

25. Mary was often ill so she wanted to be <u>healthy</u>. But she didn't know what to do.
    Mary 常常生病，所以她想要<u>健康</u>。但是她不知道該怎麼做。

26. Miss Black told Mary that she must look after herself and then do something <u>necessary</u> for her health.
    Black 小姐告訴 Mary，她必須照顧自己，並且為她的健康做一些<u>必要</u>的事。

27. Mary should do morning <u>exercises</u> and play sports.
    Mary 應該做晨間<u>體操</u>和運動。

28. Mary must eat fruit and <u>vegetables</u> and wash hands before meals.
    Mary 必須吃水果和<u>蔬菜</u>，餐前要洗手。

29. Mary shouldn't go to school without <u>breakfast</u> in the morning.
    Mary 不應該早上沒吃<u>早餐</u>就去上學。

30. Mary shouldn't watch TV too <u>much</u>, read in the sun or stay up late and so on.
    Mary 不應該看<u>太多</u>電視、在太陽底下看書、或熬夜…等等。

全新英語聽力測驗原文及參考答案
Unit 2

Ⅰ、Listen and choose the right picture.（根據你所聽到的內容,選出相應的圖片。）
（6分）

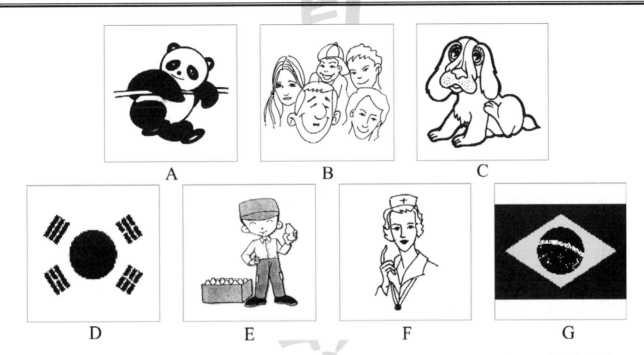

A   B   C

D   E   F   G

1. People should treat dogs as our friends because they are lovely and helpful.
   （人們應該把狗當作是我們的朋友，因為牠們很可愛也很有幫助。）
   答案：(C)

2. Is the Brazil football team the champion of the World Cup 2010?
   （巴西足球隊是 2010 世界杯的冠軍嗎？）
   答案：(G)

3. Look! The panda from Woolong is playing happily at Shanghai Wild Animal
   Park. （看！從臥龍來的熊貓在上海野生動物園快樂的玩耍。）
   答案：(A)

4. Mr Li is a milkman. He delivers milk to people in this neighborhood.
   （Li 先生是送奶工人。他為這附近的人送牛奶。）
   答案：(E)

5. Vets are doctors who take care of sick animals. （獸醫是照顧生病動物的醫生。）

　　答案：(F)

6. John made friends with many teenagers and this is a picture of them.

　　（John 與許多青少年交朋友，這是他們的照片。）

　　答案：(B)

II、Listen and choose the best response to the sentence you hear.（根據你所聽到的句子,選出最恰當的應答句。）（6分）

7. Don't forget your homework. （別忘了你的功課。）

　　(A)Yes, I will. （好，我會忘記。）　　(B)No, I won't. （不，我不會忘記。）

　　(C)Yes, I won't. （好，我不會忘記。）　　(D)No, I will. （不，我會忘記。）

　　答案：(B)

8. Where have you been during the summer holiday? （暑假期間你去了哪裡？）

　　(A)At three in the morning. （早上三點。）

　　(B)In Shanghai. （在上海。）

　　(C)With my parents. （和我父母。）

　　(D)Taiwan. （台灣。）

　　答案：(D)

9. What is your nationality? （你的國籍是？）

　　(A)Germany. （德國。）　　(B)China. （中國。）

　　(C)American. （美國人。）　　(D)Australia. （澳洲。）

　　答案：(C)

10. My brother has got a pen-friend from Canada.（我哥哥有一個來自加拿大的筆友。）

　　(A)So do I. （我也有。）　　(B)Neither do I. （我也沒有。）

　　(C)So have I. （我也有。）　　(D)Neither haven't I. （我也沒有。）

　　答案：(C)

11. Mum, shall we invite these foreign friends home?

　　（媽，我們邀請這些外國朋友來家裡好嗎？）

　　(A)That's a good idea. （那是個好主意。）

　　(B)I'm afraid you are wrong. （我恐怕你錯了。）

　　(C)That's all right. （沒關係。）

(D)You are welcome.（不客氣。）

答案：(A)

12. Give me your passport please, sir.（先生，請給我你的護照。）

(A)Here is it.（在這裡。）   (B)Here you are.（給你/在這裡。）

(C)It is here.（它在這裡。）   (D)No, I don't.（不，我不給。）

答案：(B)

Ⅲ、Listen to the dialogue and choose the best answer to the question you hear.（根據你所聽到的對話和問題,選出最恰當的答案。）（6分）

---

13. W: It is said that you made a new friend on the Internet.

（W: 聽說你在網路上交了一個新朋友。）

M: Yes, Mandy is an English engineer and she works in a French car factory.

（M: 是的，Mandy 是一位英國工程師，她在一家法國汽車工廠上班。）

Q: What nationality is Mandy?（Q: Many 的國籍是？）

(A)German.（德國人。）   (B)American.（美國人。）

(C)English.（英國人。）   (D)French.（法國人。）

答案：(C)

14. W: Excuse me, where's the teachers' office?（W: 不好意思，老師辦公室在哪裡？）

M: It's on the third floor. There is a lab on its right. On its left there is a library.

（M: 在三樓。它的右邊有一間實驗室。左邊有一間圖書館。）

Q: What is the lady looking for?（Q: 那位小姐在找甚麼？）

(A)The teachers' office.（老師辦公室。）

(B)On the third floor.（在三樓。）

(C)The library.（圖書館。）

(D)The lab.（實驗室。）

答案：(A)

15. W: Hi, Bob. I am going to hold a birthday party at home this Saturday. Are you free to come?（W: 嗨，Bob。這個星期天我要在家辦一場生日派對。你有空來嗎？）

M: I'd love to, but you know my parents will come back from their trip to Australia on Saturday morning. I need to meet them at the airport.

（M: 我想去，但是我爸媽去澳洲旅行，星期六早上就回來了。我要去機場接他們。）

W: Oh, what a pity!（W: 喔，好可惜喔！）

Q: When will the girl hold her birthday party?

（Q：那個女孩甚麼時候舉辦她的生日派對？）

(A)This Saturday.（這個星期六。）

(B)This Sunday morning.（這個星期天早上。）

(C)At the airport.（在機場。）

(D)At home.（在家。）

答案：(A)

16. W: Peter, how many girl students are there in your class?

（W：Peter，你班上有幾個女學生？）

M: There are 45 students in all. One-third of them are girls.

（M：一共有四十五個學生。三分之一是女生。）

Q: How many boy students are there in Peter's class?

（Q：Peter 的班上有多少男學生？）

(A)45.　　　　　(B)15.　　　　　(C)30.　　　　　(D)35.

答案：(C)

17. M: Welcome to Radisson. What can I do for you, Madam?

（M：歡迎來 Radisson。這位女士，我能為妳效勞嗎？）

W: I have booked a room here on the phone.（W：我電話預約了一間房間。）

M: Let me check the details. Your name please, Madam.

（M：讓我核對一下內容。女士，請教你的大名。）

W: Sophie Brown.（W：Sophie Brown。）

Q: Where does this dialogue probably take place?

（Q：這段對話大概在哪裡發生？）

(A)At a hotel.（在旅館。）　　　　　(B)At a clinic.（在診所。）

(C)In a supermarket.（在超級市場。）　(D)In a shopping mall.（在購物中心。）

答案：(A)

18. M: Where have you been during the holiday, Jane?

（M：Jane，假期期間妳去了哪裡？）

W: I have been to the US to visit my grandparents.

（W：我去美國探望我的祖父母。）

M: Oh! It must be very interesting. What did you do there?

（M：喔！那一定很有趣。妳在那裡做了些甚麼？）

W: I stayed in New York with my grandparents for two weeks. Then we went to the Disney Park in Los Angeles.

（W：我與我的祖父母在紐約待了兩個星期。然後我們去洛杉磯的迪士尼樂園。）

M: What an amazing journey!（M：好精采的旅程啊！）

Q: How many cities has Jane visited?（Q：Jane 造訪了幾個城市？）

(A)1.　　　　(B)2.　　　　(C)3.　　　　(D)4.

答案：(B)

Ⅳ、Listen to the dialogue and decide whether the following statements are True (T) or False (F).（判斷下列句子內容是否符合你所聽到的對話內容,符合的用"T"表示,不符合的用"F"表示。）（6分）

I have a pen friend called Danny. He is a boy from Australia. Danny is 22 years old. His favourite interests are taking photos and collecting coins. He works as an architect in a company. Danny starts work at nine o'clock every morning and finishes his work at a quarter past five in the afternoon. But sometimes he needs to work for a long time at home. He writes letters to me twice a month. We share happiness with each other.

我有一個筆友叫 Danny。他是來自澳洲的男孩。Danny 二十二歲。他最大的興趣就是拍照和蒐集錢幣。他在一家公司擔任建築師的工作。Danny 每天早上九點開始上班，下午五點十五分結束工作。但是有時候他需要長時在家工作。他一個月寫兩封信給我。我們分享彼此的快樂。

19. Danny is an Australian.（Danny 是澳洲人。）

答案：(T 對)

20. One of his favorite interests is playing the guitar.

（他最喜歡的興趣之一是彈吉他。）

答案：(F 錯)

21. His job is to draw plans of buildings.（他的工作是畫建築物的平面圖。）

答案：(T 對)

22. Danny has to work over 8 hours every day. （Danny 每天工作超過八小時。）

答案：(T 對)

23. He never takes work home.（他從不把工作帶回家。）

答案：(F 錯)

24. We keep in touch with each other twice a month. （我們一個月與對方聯絡兩次。）

答案：(T 對)

V、Listen and fill in the blanks.（根據你所聽到的內容,用適當的單詞完成下面的句子。每空格限填一詞。）（6分）

W: Can I help you?（W: 我能為你效勞嗎？）

M: Yes, I'd like a ticket to Thailand.（M: 是的。我想要買一張去泰國的票。）

W: For today, the third of February?（W: 是今天二月三日的票嗎？）

M: No, tomorrow morning.（M: 不，明天早上。）

W: There's a flight and you'll get there at half past five tomorrow afternoon. Is that OK?（W: 明天下午五點半有一班到泰國的班機。可以嗎？）

M: Can I have it earlier? I will have a meeting at three in the afternoon.
　（M: 我想要早一點的可以嗎？我下午三點有個會議。）

W: I'm afraid not. If you want a night flight...
　（W: 恐怕不行。如果你想要夜航班機的話...）

M: A night flight?（M: 夜航班機？）

W: Yes, with United Airlines at a quarter to ten. You'll get there at a quarter past six tomorrow morning. Is that too early?
　（W: 是的，九點四十五分的聯合航空。你將會在明天早上六點十五分抵達。會不會太早？）

M: Let me see. How much does it cost?（M: 讓我想想看。要多少錢呢？）

W: Seven hundred and eighty-six yuan. The flight number is 2316, at Gate 7, New York City Airport.
　（W: 七百八十六元。班機號碼是 2316，在紐約市機場的七號登機門。）

M: Pretty good.（M: 挺不錯的。）

W: OK. Your name, please?（W: 好。請教你的大名。）

M: My name's Jack Li.（M: 我的名字是 Jack Li。）

W: Thank you, Mr. Li. Check-in time is two hours before you get on the plane. Have a good trip.
　（W: 謝謝你，Li 先生。報到時間是登機前兩小時。祝你有個愉快的旅程。）

M: Thank you. Bye.（M: 謝謝妳，再見。）

25. The man was going to fly to <u>Thailand</u>.
    那個男人將飛往<u>泰國</u>。

26. The man wanted the flight on the date of <u>Feb. 4th</u>.
    那個男人想要搭<u>二月四日</u>的班機。

27. The number of the flight was <u>2316</u>.
    班機號碼是<u>2316</u>。

28. The flight was at Gate <u>7</u>, New York City Airport.
    班機是在紐約市機場的<u>7</u>登機門。

29. The departure time of the flight was at <u>9:45</u>.
    班機的起飛時間是<u>九點四十五分</u>。

30. The man paid <u>786</u> for the ticket.
    那個男人買機票花了<u>七百八十六元</u>。

全新英語聽力測驗原文及參考答案
Unit 3

I、Listen and choose the right picture.（根據你所聽到的內容,選出相應的圖片。）
（6分）

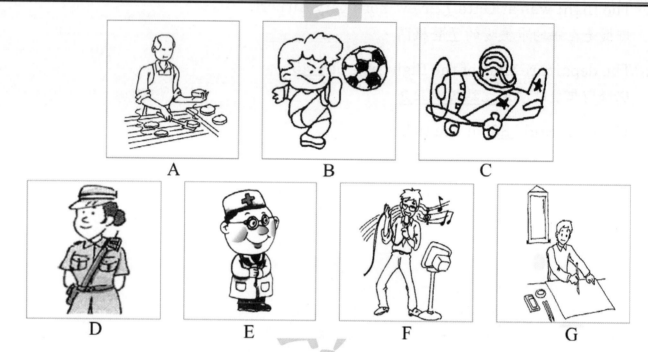

1. John is good at playing football and his ambition is to be a coach.
   （John 擅長踢足球，他的志向是當一名教練。）

   答案：(B)

2. A doctor always helps to make sick people better.
   （醫生總是幫助生病的人好起來。）

   答案：(E)

3. Tom is ready to draw a picture in the room.（Tom 準備在房間裡畫一張圖。）

   答案：(G)

4. My brother wants to be a pop singer like Jay Chou.
   （我哥哥想當一位像周杰倫一樣的流行歌手。）

   答案：(F)

5. More and more policewomen are working in the city to make our city a safe place.

（為了讓我們的城市成為一個安全的地方，有越來越多的女警在城市裡工作。）

答案：(D)

6. Yang Liwei spent about twenty-one hours in space and came back to the earth successfully in Shenzhou Ⅶ.

（楊利偉在太空度過約二十一個小時，並且搭乘神舟七號成功返回地球。）

答案：(C)

Ⅱ、Listen and choose the best response to the sentence you hear.（根據你所聽到的句子,選出最恰當的應答句。）（6分）

7. What do you think of your new job, Linda?（Linda，妳覺得妳的新工作怎麼樣？）

(A)I am a secretary.（我是秘書。）

(B)I take notes and go to meetings with my manager.

（我做記錄，並且跟我的經理去開會。）

(C)I am happy with the job because it's very interesting.

（我喜歡這份工作，因為非常有趣。）

(D)I work in an office.（我在辦公室裡上班。）

答案：(C)

8. How do you go to work every day?（你每天怎麼上班？）

(A)By subway.（搭地鐵。）

(B)In subway.（在地鐵裡。）

(C)At nine every morning.（每天早上九點。）

(D)I like my job.（我喜歡我的工作。）

答案：(A)

9. Shall I get a trolley for you?（我拿個手推車給你好嗎？）

(A)No, you can't.（不，你不能。） (B)Yes, you shall.（好，你可以。）

(C)No, thanks.（不用了，謝謝。） (D)I think so.（應該吧。）

答案：(C)

10. What does a postman do?（郵差做甚麼？）

(A)He works hard.（他努力工作。）

(B)He brings food and drinks to the customers.（他拿食物和飲料給顧客。）

(C)He delivers letters and parcels.（他遞送信件和包裹。）

(D)He draws plans of buildings.（他畫建築物的平面圖。）

答案：(C)

11. Which job do you like better, a teacher or a doctor?

（你比較喜歡哪一個工作，老師還是醫生？）

(A)Each.（每一個。）

(B)No, I don't like doctors.（不，我不喜歡醫生。）

(C)A teacher.（老師。）

(D)Yes, I do.（是的，我喜歡。）

答案：(C)

12. Sorry, I'm late because of the heavy traffic jam.

（抱歉，因為交通嚴重阻塞，所以我遲到了。）

(A)Never mind.（別介意。）　　　　(B)Not at all.（一點也不。）

(C)All right.（好。）　　　　　　　(D)That's right.（對。）

答案：(A)

Ⅲ、**Listen to the dialogue and choose the best answer to the question you hear.**

（根據你所聽到的對話和問題,選出最恰當的答案。）（6分）

---

13. M: What can I do for you?（M: 我能為妳服務嗎？）

W: I want to post a letter, but I don't know the postage.

（W: 我想寄一封信，但我不知道郵資。）

Q: Where is the girl?（Q: 女孩在哪裡？）

(A)In the bookstore.（在書店。）　　(B)In a police station.（在警察局。）

(C)At a canteen.（在學校餐廳。）　　(D)In a post office.（在郵局。）

答案：(D)

14. M: How do you go to school?（M: 妳怎麼上學？）

W: Usually on foot, but when it rains I'll take a taxi.

（W: 通常是走路，但是下雨的時候我會搭計程車。）

Q: How does the girl go to school when it is sunny?

（Q: 晴天的時候，女孩怎麼上學？）

(A)By car.（搭車。）　　　　　　　(B)By underground.（搭地鐵。）

(C)By taxi.（搭計程車。）　　　　　(D)On foot.（走路。）

答案：(D)

15. W: What time is it now? I have a meeting at 2 o'clock.

（W: 現在幾點？我兩點有個會議。）

M: Don't worry. It's only half past one.（M: 別擔心。現在才一點半。）

Q: When will the meeting begin?（Q: 會議甚麼時候開始？）

(A)At 1:00.（一點。）   (B)At 1:30.（一點半。）

(C)At 2:00.（兩點。）   (D)At 2:30.（兩點半。）

答案：(C)

16. M: Jack was a teacher many years ago, wasn't he?

（M: Jack 在多年前是一位老師，對嗎？）

W: No, he worked in a company. But now he works as an ambulance worker.

（W: 不，他在一家公司上班。但是他現在是救護車工作人員。）

Q: What's Jack's job now?（Q: Jack 現在的工作是甚麼？）

(A)A teacher.（老師。）

(B)An ambulance worker.（救護車工作人員。）

(C)An office worker.（辦公族。）

(D)An architect.（建築師。）

答案：(B)

17. W: Do you live near school, Bill?（W: Bill，你住學校附近嗎？）

M: Yes, it takes me 5 minutes to walk to school.

（M: 是的，我走路去學校只要五分鐘。）

Q: Does Mark live near or far away from school?（Q: Mark 住得離學校近還是遠？）

(A)He lives near the school.（他住學校附近。）

(B)He lives far away from the school.（他住得離學校很遠。）

(C)Yes, he does.（是的，他是。）

(D)No, he doesn't.（不，他不是。）

答案：(A)

18. M: Have you prepared for the class meeting?（M: 班級會議妳準備好了嗎？）

W: Yes, everything is ready. We've got 25 chairs in the classroom.

（W: 都準備好了。教室裡有二十五張椅子。）

M: I'm afraid we need 5 more for the teachers.

（M: 恐怕我們還需要五張椅子給老師。）

Q: How many people will come to the class meeting?

（Q: 有多少人會來班級會議？）

(A)25.   (B)30.   (C)35.   (D)20.

答案：(B)

IV、Listen to the dialogue and decide whether the following statements are True (T) or False (F). (判斷下列句子內容是否符合你所聽到的對話內容，符合的用"T"表示，不符合的用"F"表示。)（6分）

Once a rich man went to the sea for his summer holidays. He asked his housekeeper to post him all the letters that he would receive when he was away. The housekeeper agreed to do that. The man had a good rest. A month passed but he received no letters. He thought it strange and rang up his housekeeper.

從前有一個有錢人到海邊過暑假。他要求管家把他離家時無法收到的信都寄給他。管家答應了。那個人便放心地好好休息。一個月過去了，他卻沒收到信。他覺得很奇怪，所以打電話給他的管家。

"Why didn't you post my letters?"

"Because you didn't leave me the key to the letter box," his housekeeper replied.

「為什麼你沒寄信給我？」「因為你沒把信箱鑰匙留給我。」管家回答。

The man said sorry and promised to send back the key. A few days later he put the key into an envelope, wrote down his address on it and posted the letter. Another month passed but still he did not receive the letters.

那個人說了聲抱歉並且答應要把鑰匙寄回去。過了幾天後，他把鑰匙放進信封裡，在上面寫下他的地址後把信寄了出去。又一個月過去了，他仍然沒收到信。

When he returned home at the end of the month, he spoke angrily to his housekeeper.

他在那個月的月底回家，他很生氣地對管家說話。

"But what could I do?" asked the poor housekeeper. "The key which you posted was in the locked letter box, too."

「但是我能怎麼辦？」可憐的管家問他，「你寄來的鑰匙也在被鎖住的信箱裡啊。」

19. The man who went to the sea for his summer holidays was rich.

（去海邊度過暑假的那個男人很富有。）

答案：(T 對)

20. He asked his housekeeper to post him all the letters when he was not at home.

（他要求他的管家在他不在家的時候，把所有的信都寄給他。）

答案：(T 對)

21. The housekeeper did not promise to post all the letters.（管家不答應寄信。）

答案：(F 錯)

22. The man took the key to the letter box with him when he left home.

（男人離家的時候帶著信箱鑰匙。）

答案：(T 對)

23. The man did not receive the letters until the next month.

（男人直到下個月才收到信。）

答案：(F 錯)

24. When the man returned home, he was unhappy to speak to his housekeeper.

（男人回家的時候，他很不高興地對著管家說話。）

答案：(T 對)

Ⅴ、**Listen and fill in the blanks.**（根據你所聽到的內容,用適當的單詞完成下面的句子。每空格限填一詞。）（6分）

Jenny always wanted to be a singer. Music was the most important thing in her life, but to tell you the truth, she has a terrible voice. She took lessons for many years, but her voice didn't become better. In fact, it just got louder.

Jenny 一直想當歌手。音樂在她的生活中是最重要的，但老實跟你說，她的聲音很糟。她上了很多年的課，但是她的聲音卻無法變好。事實上，只是變得比較大聲。

Her teacher finally gave up and stopped her lessons. But Jenny didn't want to stop. One day, she decided to give a concert and invited her teacher to attend. The teacher was very worried about what to say after the concert. She knew it would be a bad one. What should she do?

她的老師最後放棄並且停了她的課。但是 Jenny 不想停課。有一天，她決定辦一個演唱會並且請她的老師來參加。老師非常擔心演唱會後該說些甚麼。她知道那會很糟。她該怎麼辦呢？

25. Jenny always wanted to be a <u>singer</u>.
    Jenny 一直想當<u>歌手</u>。

26. Music was the most <u>important</u> thing in her life, but she has a terrible voice.
    音樂在她生活中是最<u>重要的</u>，但是她的聲音很糟。

27. She <u>took</u> lessons for many years.
    她<u>上了</u>很多年的課。

28. Her voice didn't become <u>better</u>. In fact, it just got louder.
    她的聲音沒有變得<u>更好</u>。事實上只是變得比較大聲。

29. The teacher was very <u>worried</u> about what to say after the concert.
    老師非常<u>擔心</u>演唱會後該說些甚麼。

30. She knew it <u>would</u> be a bad one.
    她知道那<u>將</u>會很糟。

全新英語聽力測驗原文及參考答案

Unit 4

I、Listen and choose the right picture.（根據你所聽到的內容,選出相應的圖片。）
（6分）

1. Brad is a removal man who works in a removal company.
   （Brad 是一個在搬家公司工作的搬運工人。）

   答案：(B)

2. There is a computer in my study.（我書房裡有一台電腦。）

   答案：(A)

3. My boss lives in a villa in the suburbs.（我老闆住在郊區的一棟別墅。）

   答案：(G)

4. Mr. Black walks his puppy twice a day.（Black 先生每天帶他的小狗散步兩次。）

   答案：(E)

5. In the Maths lesson yesterday, Mr. Liu asked us a difficult question.
   （在昨天的數學課中，Liu 先生問了我們一道很難的問題。）

   答案：(F)

6. You'd better put some flowers or green plants at home. It's good for your health.
    （你最好在家擺一些花或是綠色植物。這有益你的健康。）
    答案：(D)

II、Listen and choose the best response to the sentence you hear.（根據你所聽到的句子,選出最恰當的應答句。）（6分）

7. Why not go for a walk?（為什麼不去散步呢？）
    (A)Good idea.（好主意。）   (B)No, I can't.（不，我不能。）
    (C)It's sunny.（今天是晴天。）   (D)It's good for you.（這對你有益。）
    答案：(A)

8. How long have you lived in your new neighbourhood?
    （你住在新的鄰里街坊有多久了？）
    (A)Two months ago.（兩個月以前。）
    (B)For two months.（有兩個月了。）
    (C)Since two months.（自兩個月以前開始。）
    (D)In two months.（在兩個月以內。）
    答案：(B)

9. What is Uncle Li?（Li 叔叔是做甚麼的？）
    (A)He is thirty years old.（他三十歲。）
    (B)He is tall and thin.（他又高又瘦。）
    (C)He works hard.（他努力工作。）
    (D)He is a police officer.（他是警察。）
    答案：(D)

10. You did very well in the English spelling contest.
    你在英語拼音比賽上表現得很好。
    (A)Thank you.（謝謝你。）   (B)No, I didn't.（不，我表現得不好。）
    (C)Don't say so.（別這麼說。）   (D)I am not good.（我不好。）
    答案：(A)

11. Would you mind if I open the door? It's really hot inside.
    （你介意我把門打開嗎？這裡真的很熱。）
    (A)You are welcome.（不客氣。）   (B)With pleasure.（我的榮幸。）

(C)Of course not.（當然不介意。）　　　　(D)I agree.（我同意。）

答案：(C)

12. What's the matter with you?（你怎麼了？）

(A)I'm a student.（我是學生。）

(B)I am reading a newspaper.（我在看報紙。）

(C)I have a bad headache.（我頭很痛。）

(D)I have been to the U.S.A. before.（我以前去過美國。）

答案：(C)

Ⅲ、Listen to the dialogue and choose the best answer to the question you hear.
（根據你所聽到的對話和問題,選出最恰當的答案。）（6分）

13. M: You have moved into a new flat. Congratulations, Mary!

　　（M: 妳搬進新公寓了。Mary, 恭喜妳！）

W: Thanks, John.（W: John, 謝謝你。）

M: How many rooms are there in your new flat, Mary?

　　（M: Mary，妳的新公寓有幾個房間？）

W: I have a big sitting room, a kitchen, a bathroom, a bedroom and a study.

　　（W: 我有一個大起居室，一個廚房，一個廁所，一個臥室和一個書房。）

Q: How many rooms are there in Mary's new flat?

　　（Q: Mary 的新公寓有幾個房間？）

(A)4.　　　　　(B)5.　　　　　(C)6.　　　　　(D)7.

答案：(B)

14. M: Where do you like to live, in the city center or in the suburbs?

　　（M: 妳喜歡住在哪裡？市中心還是郊區？）

W: Although it's convenient to live in the city center, I'd rather live a quiet life in
　　the suburbs.（W: 雖然住在市中心很方便，但是我寧願在郊區過著安靜的生活。）

M: I agree with you.（M: 我同意。）

Q: Where does the girl like to live, in the city center or in the suburbs?

　　（Q: 女孩喜歡住在哪裡？市中心還是郊區？）

(A)In the city center.（市中心。）　　　　(B)In the suburbs.（郊區。）

(C)Both.（兩個都喜歡。）　　　　(D)Neither.（兩個都不喜歡。）

答案：(B)

15. M: Madam, where do you want the cupboard?
    （M: 女士，這個碗櫃妳要擺在哪裡？）

    W: Put it near the shelf, please.（W: 請放在書架附近。）

    M: What about the picture?（M: 這張圖呢？）

    W: Next to the clock on the wall. And I want the fridge on the right by the window.（W: 時鐘旁邊的牆上。我還想把電冰箱放在右邊的窗戶旁。）

    Q: Where does the woman want the picture?（Q: 女人想要把那張圖放在哪裡？）

    (A)Near the shelf.（靠近書架。）　　　(B)Next to the clock.（時鐘的旁邊。）

    (C)By the window.（窗戶邊。）　　　(D)On the sofa.（沙發上。）

    答案：(B)

16. W: You look tired. What did you do last weekend?
    （W: 你看起來很累。你上個周末做了甚麼？）

    M: On Saturday, I didn't finish my homework until 11:00. Then I watered flowers.（M: 星期六我寫功課寫到十一點。然後去澆花。）

    W: And what did you do on Sunday?（W: 你星期天做了甚麼？）

    M: I helped my father clean the car.（M: 我幫我爸爸清理車子。）

    Q: What did the boy do on Sunday?（Q: 男孩星期天做了甚麼？）

    (A)He did his homework.（他做功課。）

    (B)He watered flowers.（他澆花。）

    (C)He cleaned the car with his father.（他跟他爸爸一起清理車子。）

    (D)He watched TV.（他看電視。）

    答案：(C)

17. W: What can I do for you?（W: 我能為你效勞嗎？）

    M: I'm looking for a wooden bookshelf.（M: 我想找一個木製的書架。）

    W: We have many styles of wooden bookshelves. Walk around and have a look, sir.（W: 我們有非常多樣式的木製書架。先生，你可以到處走走看看。）

    Q: Where does the dialogue probably take place?
    （Q: 這段對話大概發生在甚麼地方？）

    (A)At a toy shop.（在玩具店。）　　　(B)At a cloth shop.（在服裝店。）

    (C)At a CD shop.（在 CD 音樂行。）　　(D)At a furniture shop.（在家具店。）

    答案：(D)

18. M: What's your plan for the summer holidays, May?
    （M: May，妳暑假的計畫是甚麼？）

W: I will go to Lijiang.（W: 我要去麗江。）

M: That's a wonderful place for traveling. Who will you go there with, your father or your mother?

（M: 那是個旅行的好地方。妳要跟誰去，妳父親還是妳母親？）

W: Neither of them. I'll go with my friend.（W: 都不是。我要跟我朋友去。）

Q: Who will May go to Lijiang with?（Q: May 要跟誰去麗江？）

(A)Her father.（她父親。）

(B)Her mother.（她母親。）

(C)Her friend.（她朋友。）

(D)Her parents.（她的父母。）

答案：(C)

Ⅳ、Listen to the dialogue and decide whether the following statements are True (T) or False (F).（判斷下列句子內容是否符合你所聽到的對話內容,符合的用"T"表示,不符合的用"F"表示。）（6分）

Mr. Wang has a ten-year-old boy, Tom. Tom likes playing football and he always helps other people. But he is a careless boy. Yesterday Mr. Wang had to leave home for a while. He said to Tom, "Be good at home. I'll come back in 10 minutes." Tom watched TV for a while and then he played with matches and started a fire. The small fire became a big fire soon and Tom was very frightened. He called a fire station.

Wang 先生有個十歲的男孩 Tom。Tom 喜歡踢足球而且他總是幫助他人。但是他是一個粗心的男孩。昨天 Wang 先生要離家一會兒。他對 Tom 說：「乖乖在家。我十分鐘後回來。」Tom 看了一會兒電視，然後玩火柴還引起火災。火勢很快的就由小變大，Tom 非常害怕。他打電話給消防隊。

"Fire station, can I help you?" one of the firemen picked up the telephone and said.

「這裡是消防隊，我能為你服務嗎？」一位消防員接了電話說。

"Fire! Fire!" 「火災！火災！」

"Where is it?" asked the fireman. 「在哪裡？」消防員問。

"In my house! Come quickly, or it will be burnt down!"

「在我家！趕快來，要不然就要燒毀了！」

"But in what place is the fire?" asked the fireman.

「火災發生在甚麼地方？」消防員問。

"In the kitchen!" answered Tom. 「在廚房！」Tom 回答。

"Yes, but how can we get to your place?"

「好。但是我們要怎麼去你住的地方呢？」

"Haven't you got a fire-engine to come here?" was the surprised answer.

「你們難道沒有消防車可以來這兒嗎？」這是一個多麼令人驚訝的回答啊。

19. Tom is a twelve-year-old boy. (Tom 是一個十二歲的男孩。)
    答案：(F 錯)

20. Tom doesn't like any ball games. (Tom 不喜歡任何球類運動。)
    答案：(F 錯)

21. Although Tom likes helping others, he is not careful.
    （雖然 Tom 喜歡幫助他人，但是他不細心。）
    答案：(T 對)

22. Tom started a fire in his bedroom after his father left.
    （在他父親離開之後，Tom 在他的臥室引起火災。）
    答案：(F 錯)

23. The firemen couldn't come because there was no fire engine.
    （消防員來不了是因為沒有消防車。）
    答案：(F 錯)

24. What the fireman wanted to know was Tom's address.
    （消防員想知道的是 Tom 的地址。）
    答案：(T 對)

V、Listen and fill in the blanks.（根據你所聽到的內容,用適當的單詞完成下面的句子。每空格限填一詞。）（6分）

W: Hello, Sunny Bay Agency. What can I do for you?
（W: 哈囉，這裡是 Sunny Bay Agency。我能為你服務嗎？）

M: I'm David Black, from America. Now I'm studying here. I'd like to rent a flat with my classmates.

（M: 我是來自美國的 David Black。我現在在這裡唸書。我想和我同學一起租一間公寓房。）

W: What kind of flat would you like?（W: 你喜歡怎樣的公寓？）

M: I want to live in the city center. It's more convenient.

（W: 我想住在市中心。會比較方便。）

W: We just have a flat here, in the center of Shanghai. The building has six storeys and it's on the third floor. It has a sitting room, a dining-room, three bedrooms and two bathrooms.

（W: 我們剛好在上海市中心有一間公寓房。它在一棟六層樓公寓的三樓。它有一個起居室，一個餐廳，三間臥室和兩間廁所。）

M: That sounds good!（M: 聽起來很不錯！）

W: And it is very convenient. It's just near No.1 Underground and it's four minutes' walk to the People's Square.

（W: 而且它非常方便。它剛好靠近一號地鐵，走路四分鐘就到人民廣場。）

M: How much should I pay per month?（M: 我一個月要付多少錢？）

W: It's a bit expensive. 2,500 yuan per month.（W: 這有點貴。一個月兩千五百元。）

M: I will reply to you tomorrow, OK?（M: 我明天給你回覆，好嗎？）

W: No problem. My phone number is 63240081.

（W: 沒問題。我的電話號碼是 63240081。）

M: Pardon?（M: 請再說一次好嗎？）

W: 63240081.（W: 63240081。）

25. David is from <u>America</u>.
   David 來自<u>美國</u>。

26. He wants to live in the city center, because it's more <u>convenient</u>.
   他想住在市中心，因為那比較<u>方便</u>。

27. Sunny Bay Agency has a flat with a sitting room, a <u>dining</u> room, three bedrooms and two bathrooms.
   Sunny Bay Agency 有一間公寓房，配備一個起居室，一個<u>餐廳</u>，三間臥室和兩間廁所。

28. The flat is about four <u>minutes'</u> walk to the People's Square.
   從那間公寓走去人民廣場大約要四<u>分鐘</u>。

29. David should pay <u>2,500</u> yuan per month.
   David 每個月要付<u>兩千五百元</u>。

30. The agent's telephone number is <u>63240081</u>.
   仲介的電話號碼是 <u>63240081</u>。

全新英語聽力測驗原文及參考答案

Unit 5

I、Listen and choose the right picture.（根據你所聽到的內容,選出相應的圖片。）
（6分）

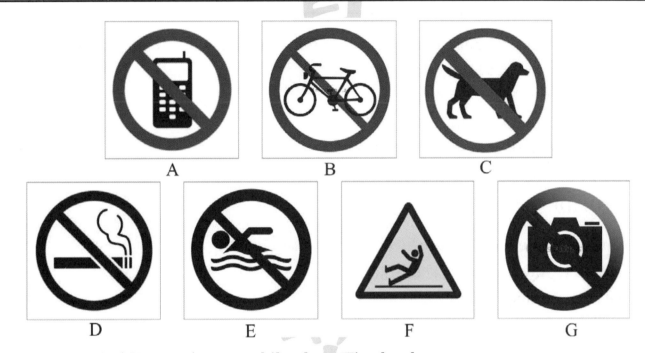

1. Keep quiet! You can't use mobile phones in the theatre.
    （保持安靜！你不可以在電影院裡使用行動電話。）
    答案：(A)

2. Can't you see the sign? It says no cycling.
    （你沒看見那個標示嗎？上面寫著不准騎腳踏車。）
    答案：(B)

3. Watch your steps! It's quite slippery here.（注意你的腳步！這裡相當的滑。）
    答案：(F)

4. Taking photos is not allowed in the museum.（在博物館裡拍照是不被允許的。）
    答案：(G)

5. Don't let your puppy enter the green grass.
    不要讓你的小狗進入草地。

答案：(C)

6.　You mustn't swim in the river. It's too dangerous.
（你不可以在河裡游泳。太危險了。）
答案：(E)

II、Listen and choose the best response to the sentence you hear.（根據你所聽到的句子,選出最恰當的應答句。）（6分）

7.　The sign tells us what we mustn't do. What sign is it?
（這個標示告訴我們甚麼事不能做。那是甚麼標示？）
(A)A direction sign.（方向標示。）
(B)An information sign.（訊息標示。）
(C)An instruction sign.（指示標示。）
(D)A warning sign.（警告標示。）
答案：(D)

8.　Can I pick the flowers here?（我可以在這裡摘花嗎？）
(A)Sorry, you mustn't.（抱歉，不行。）
(B)Yes, you may.（是的，你也許可以。）
(C)There are flowers in the park.（公園裡有花。）
(D)Flowers are nice.（花很好看。）
答案：(A)

9.　Mum, I got an F for my English.（媽，我英文得了個 F。）
(A)I will take your advice.（我會採納你的建議。）
(B)That's good.（那很好。）
(C)You should study harder.（你該更努力一點。）
(D)I think so.（應該吧。）
答案：(C)

10.　You have broken the school record for the 110-meter hurdle. Congratulations!
（你已經打破 110 公尺跳欄的學校記錄。恭喜你！）
(A)Thank you.（謝謝你。）　　　　　(B)Don't say so.（別這麼說。）
(C)No, I don't.（不，我沒有。）　　　(D)That's all right.（沒關係。）
答案：(A)

11. Let's plant more trees on Tree Planting Day!（我們在植樹節多種一些樹吧！）
    (A)Good idea.（好主意。）　　　　　(B)I think so, too.（我也這麼想。）
    (C)Yes, I will.（好的，我會。）　　　(D)I'm glad.（我很高興。）
    答案：(A)

12. How soon will you finish your work, Jim?（Jim，你多快可以完成你的工作？）
    (A)For at least one hour.（至少持續一小時。）
    (B)In one hour.（一小時以內。）
    (C)At one o'clock.（一點。）
    (D)By one hour.（差一小時。）
    答案：(B)

Ⅲ、Listen to the dialogue and choose the best answer to the question you hear.
（根據你所聽到的對話和問題,選出最恰當的答案。）（6分）

---

13. M: Can I smoke here?（M: 我可以在這裡抽菸嗎？）
    W: Look at the sign on the wall. It says "No smoking".
       （W: 看看牆上的標示。上面寫著「禁止吸煙」）
    Q: Can the man smoke here?（Q: 這個男人可以在這裡抽菸嗎?）
    (A)Yes, he can.（是的，他可以。）　　　(B)No, he can't.（不，他不可以。）
    (C)Yes, he does.（是的，他抽菸。）　　(D)No, he doesn't.（不，他不抽菸。）
    答案：(B)

14. M: Hi, this is John. How's everything going on with you?
       （M: 嗨，我是 John。妳好嗎?）
    W: Shh... Don't talk loudly here. Haven't you seen the sign "Silence" over there?
       Everyone else is reading here. (W: 噓...別在這裡大聲說話。你沒看到那裡有個
       "請安靜" 的標示嗎? 每個人都在這兒讀書。）
    Q: Where does the dialogue probably take place?
       （Q: 這段對話大概發生在甚麼地方?）
    (A)At home.（在家。）　　　　　　　(B)In the hospital.（在醫院。）
    (C)At the zoo.（在動物園。）　　　　(D)In the reading room.（在閱覽室。）
    答案：(D)

15. M: Mrs Fraser, can we have an interview right now?
       （M: Fraser 女士，我們現在可以來進行面談嗎?）

W: Sure. (W: 當然可以。)

M: What job do you do? (M: 妳從事甚麼工作?)

W: I work for the SPCA. We protect the animals and help homeless animals find their new homes.

（W: 我在 SPCA 工作。我們保護動物並幫助流浪動物找到牠們的新家。）

M: When did you start working as an SPCA officer?

（M: 妳什麼時候開始擔任 SPCA 的工作人員?）

W: Three years ago. (W: 三年前。)

Q: What does the SPCA protect? (Q: SPCA 保護甚麼?)

(A)An SPCA officer. (SPCA 工作人員。)

(B)Homeless children. (無家可歸的兒童。)

(C)Homeless animals. (流浪動物。)

(D)Three years ago. (三年前。)

答案：(C)

16. M: How much are the apples? (M: 這些蘋果多少錢?)

W: 5 yuan a kilo. (W: 一公斤五元。)

M: What about the watermelon? (M: 西瓜呢?)

W: For the small ones, 10 yuan each and 15 yuan each for the big ones.

（W: 小的一個十元，大的一個十五元。）

M: Would you please give me two kilos of apples and one big watermelon?

（M: 請給我兩公斤蘋果和一個大西瓜。）

Q: How much will the man pay for the fruit? (Q: 這個男人花多少錢買水果?)

(A)10.　　　　(B)15.　　　　(C)20.　　　　(D)25.

答案：(D)

17. W: What do you like to do in the future? (W: 你未來想做甚麼?)

M: I'd like to be a police officer. I want to catch thieves and help make the city safe. It's interesting. What about you?

（M: 我想當警察。我想逮捕小偷並協助維持城市的安全。這很有趣。妳呢?）

W: I want to be a doctor. I like to help others.

（W: 我想當醫生。我喜歡幫助他人。）

Q: What does the girl want to be in the future?

（Q: 女孩未來想當甚麼?）

(A)A police officer. (警察。)　　　　(B)To catch thieves. (逮捕小偷。)

(C)To help others.（幫助其他人。）　　　　(D)A doctor.（醫生。）

答案：(D)

18. W: Excuse me, what day is it today?（W: 抱歉，今天星期幾?）

M: It's Saturday.（M: 今天星期六。）

Q: What day was it the day before yesterday?（Q: 前天星期幾?）

(A)Wednesday.（星期三。）　　　　(B)Thursday.（星期四。）

(C)Tuesday.（星期二。）　　　　(D)Friday.（星期五。）

答案：(B)

Ⅳ、Listen to the dialogue and decide whether the following statements are True (T) or False (F).（判斷下列句子內容是否符合你所聽到的對話內容,符合的用"T"表示,不符合的用"F"表示。）（6分）

Last Saturday Mr White and his wife went to the city centre. They spent a nice day in the downtown and got home very late. Mr White opened the front door and went into the house. It was very dark, so Mr White turned on the lights. On the way upstairs Mrs White said, "Listen, I can hear someone in the bedroom." So they went downstairs again and stood quietly outside the room, listening carefully. "Yes, you're right," said Mr White. "There are two boys. They are talking!" Then he called out, "Who is there?" But nobody answered. Mr White opened the door and quickly turned on the light. Then they burst out laughing. The radio was still on. "Oh, dear!" he said, "I forgot to turn off the radio this morning."

上星期六 White 先生和他的太太去市中心。他們一整天在鬧區玩得很開心，很晚才回家。White 先生打開前門進入屋內。屋裡非常暗，所以 White 先生把燈打開。White 太太要往樓梯走的時候，她說：「你聽，我聽見臥室裡有人。」於是他們又下樓，安靜的站在房間外面，仔細地聽。「是的，你是對的。」White 先生說。「裡面有兩個男孩，他們正在說話！」然後他大叫了出來：「是誰在那裡？」但是沒人回答。White 先生開了門，很快的把燈打開。結果他們都笑了出來。收音機還是開著的。「喔，親愛的！」他說，「今天早上我忘了關收音機了。」

---

19. Mr and Mrs White went to the city centre on Saturday.

（White 先生和太太星期六去市中心。）

答案：(T 對)

20. When Mr and Mrs White returned home late, it was very dark in the room.

（當 White 先生和太太很晚回家的時候，房間裡非常暗。）

答案：(T 對)

21. Mr and Mrs White's bedroom is on the ground floor.

（White 先生和太太的臥室在一樓。）

答案：(T 對)

22. On the way to the front door, they heard someone talking.

（在往前門的路上，他們聽見有人說話。）

答案：(F 錯)

23. Two boys broke into the house during the day time and stayed there.

（兩個男孩在白天的時候闖入他們家，並待在那兒。）

答案：(F 錯)

24. Mr White forgot to turn off the TV in the morning.

White 先生早上忘了關電視。

答案：(F 錯)

V、Listen and fill in the blanks.（根據你所聽到的內容,用適當的單詞完成下面的句子。每空格限填一詞。）（6分）

All students need to have good study habits. Good study habits are very important. When you have them, you learn things quickly. You also remember them easily. For example, a living room is not a good place to study in, because it is too noisy. You need to study in a quiet place. A quiet place will help you concentrate (集中). When you study, don't think about other things at the same time. Only think about your homework. If you do this, you will make fewer mistakes. Every student should have good habits. If you do not have them, try to learn them. If yours are already good, try to make them better.

所有的學生都需要有好的讀書習慣。好的讀書習慣非常重要。只要你有了好的讀書習慣，你會學得很快。你也很容易記住這些習慣。舉例來說，客廳不是讀書的好地方，因為那兒太吵。你需要在安靜的地方讀書。安靜的地方可以幫助你集中精神。當你唸書的時候，不要同時想其它的事。只要想你的功課就好。這樣的話，你犯的錯就會比較少。每一個學生都應該有好的習慣。如果你沒有，試著學會。如果你的習慣已經很好了，試著讓它們更好。

25. Good study habits are very <u>important</u>.
    好的讀書習慣非常<u>重要</u>。

26. When you have good study habits, you learn things <u>quickly</u>.
    當你有了好的讀書習慣，你學東西會<u>很快</u>。

27. When you study, don't think about <u>other</u> things at the same time.
    當你讀書的時候，不要同時想<u>其它的</u>的事。

28. If you do this, you will make <u>fewer</u> mistakes.
    如果你這樣做的話，你犯的錯會<u>比較少</u>。

29. Every student should <u>have</u> good habits.
    每一個學生都應該<u>有</u>好的習慣。

30. If your study habits are already good, try to make them <u>better</u>.
    如果你的讀書習慣已經很好了，試著讓它們<u>更好</u>。

全新英語聽力測驗原文及參考答案

Unit 6

> I、Listen and choose the right picture.（根據你所聽到的內容,選出相應的圖片。）
> （6分）

A   B   C

D   E   F   G

1. You'd better drink water instead of beverages after sports.
   （運動之後你最好喝水而不是喝飲料。）

   答案：(A)

2. Fast food like hamburgers is not good for our health.
   （像漢堡之類的速食對我們的健康不好。）

   答案：(E)

3. We should do morning exercises every day to keep healthy.
   （為了保持健康,我們應該每天做晨間運動。）

   答案：(G)

4. Although it's cool to have a bath under cold water in summer, it is harmful to people.（雖然夏天沖冷水澡很涼快,但是那對人們有害。）

   答案：(C)

5. Tom is angry with his little sister because she broke his glasses.
（Tom 對他妹妹很生氣，因為她打破了他的眼鏡。）
答案：(F)

6. It is a good habit to wash hands before we eat.（飯前洗手是好習慣。）
答案：(B)

II、Listen and choose the best response to the sentence you hear.（根據你所聽到的句子,選出最恰當的應答句。）（6分）

---

7. I will have an important math test tomorrow.（我明天有一場重要的數學測驗。）
   (A)How do you do?（你好嗎？）　　　(B)Good luck!（祝你好運！）
   (C)Never mind.（別介意。）　　　(D)That's nothing.（那沒甚麼。）
   答案：(B)

8. I think we should have more vegetables and fruits.
   （我覺得我們應該多吃蔬菜水果。）
   (A)So should I.（我也應該。）　　　(B)Neither should I.（我也不應該。）
   (C)I think so, too.（我也這麼認為。）　　　(D)I think not.（我認為不是。）
   答案：(C)

9. Could you please give me the notebook?（請給我那本筆記本可以嗎？）
   (A)Yes, I could.（好，我可以。）　　　(B)No, I couldn't.（不，我不行。）
   (C)I haven't.（我沒有。）　　　(D)Here you are.（給你。）
   答案：(D)

10. I wonder if I could possibly use your bicycle.（我不知道我可不可以用你的腳踏車。）
    (A)Yes, you can.（是的，你可以。）
    (B)No, you can't.（不，你不行。）
    (C)Sorry, I don't have time.（抱歉，我沒時間。）
    (D)Sure, go ahead.（當然，拿去吧。）
    答案：(D)

11. You are late again.（你又遲到了。）
    (A)Yes, I am.（是的，我是。）
    (B)I'm sorry, Miss Lin. I will come earlier next time.
       （Lin 小姐，對不起。我下次一定早點來。）
    (C)It doesn't matter.（沒關係。）

(D)I think you are right.（我認為你是對的。）

答案：(B)

12. How can I keep healthy?（我該怎麼保持健康呢？）

(A)You'd better have more chocolate.（你最好多吃巧克力。）

(B)You'd better eat more healthy food.（你最好吃更健康的食物。）

(C)You'd better watch more TV.（你最好多看電視。）

(D)You'd better do less exercise.（你最好少做運動。）

答案：(B)

Ⅲ、**Listen to the dialogue and choose the best answer to the question you hear.**
（根據你所聽到的對話和問題,選出最恰當的答案。）（6分）

13. W: Why don't you talk to Rose about it? She's free now.

（W：你為什麼不告訴 Rose 這件事？她現在有空。）

M: OK. I'll do that.（M：好。我會去說。）

Q: How is Rose now?（Q：Rose 現在怎麼樣？）

(A)She's not busy.（她不忙。）

(B)She is busy.（她很忙。）

(C)She is ill in the hospital.（她生病了在醫院。）

(D)She is talking.（她在說話。）

答案：(A)

14. M: I used to eat a lot of ice cream and chocolate, because I liked sweet food.

（M：我以前吃很多冰淇淋和巧克力，因為我喜歡甜食。）

W: But it's not a healthy diet to eat too much ice cream.

（W：但是吃太多冰淇淋是不健康的飲食習慣。）

M: I know now. I have changed my eating habit.

（M：我現在知道了。我已經改變我的飲食習慣了。）

W: Are you still eating a lot of ice cream and chocolate?

（W：你現在仍然吃很多冰淇淋和巧克力嗎？）

M: No, not as much as I used to. Now I eat a lot of fruit and vegetables every day.

（M：不像我以前吃得那麼多。我現在每天吃很多水果和蔬菜。）

Q: What does the man eat now?（Q：那個男人現在吃甚麼？）

(A)A lot of fruit and vegetables.（很多水果和蔬菜。）

(B)Some ice cream.（一些冰淇淋。）

(C)Some chocolate.（一些巧克力。）

(D)All the above.（以上全部。）

答案：(D)

15. W: Hi, Michael. Can I ask you some questions?

（W: 嗨，Michael。我能問你一些問題嗎？）

M: Sure.（M: 當然可以。）

W: Do you like your job?（W: 你喜歡你的工作嗎？）

M: Of course.（M: 當然。）

W: How long have you worked as a teacher?（W: 你當老師有多久了？）

M: I started my job in 1997 when I was twenty-four and have worked for about fourteen years.

（M: 一九七七年我二十四歲的時候開始工作，而且已經做了有十四年了。）

Q: How old was Michael when he started his work?（Q: Michael 幾歲開始工作？）

(A)22.　　　　　(B)24.　　　　　(C)38.　　　　　(D)48.

答案：(B)

16. M: There is going to be a table tennis game this evening, Mary. Shall we watch it together?

（M: Mary，今天晚上有一場桌球賽。我們一起去看好嗎？）

W: Sorry, I like football.（W: 抱歉，我喜歡足球。）

Q: Why won't Mary go to watch the table tennis game?

（Q: 為什麼 Mary 不去看桌球賽？）

(A)Because she doesn't like table tennis.（因為她不喜歡桌球。）

(B)Because she will watch a football game.（因為她要看足球賽。）

(C)Because she will watch a basketball game.（因為她要看籃球賽。）

(D)Because she will visit Nanpu Bridge.（因為她要造訪南浦大橋。）

答案：(A)

17. W: Would you like some tea or coffee?（W: 你想要喝點茶或咖啡嗎？）

M: I prefer tea to coffee. But today I've had enough.

（M: 我喜歡茶勝過咖啡。但是今天我已經喝得夠多了。）

Q: Which does the man want now, tea or coffee?

（Q: 那個男人現在想要喝茶還是咖啡？）

(A)Tea.（茶。）　　　　　　　　　(B)Coffee.（咖啡。）

(C)Both.（都要。）　　　　　　　　　　(D)Neither.（都不要）

答案：(D)

18. W: Is that Mark speaking?（W: 是 Mark 嗎？）

M: Speaking.（M: 我是。）

W: This is Barbara. I'm planning a surprise birthday party. Are you free on Saturday afternoon?

（W: 我是 Barbara。我正計畫一個驚喜的生日派對。你星期六下午有空嗎？）

Q: Where are they talking?（Q: 他們在哪裡說話？）

(A)In the classroom.（在教室。）

(B)At Mark's home.（在 Mark 家。）

(C)On the phone.（電話中。）

(D)At the birthday party.（在生日派對。）

答案：(C)

IV、**Listen to the dialogue and decide whether the following statements are True (T) or False (F).**（判斷下列句子內容是否符合你所聽到的對話內容,符合的用"T"表示,不符合的用"F"表示。）（6分）

Tea is one of the most popular beverages all over the world. It has a long history. But tea does not mean the same thing to everyone.

茶是世界上最受歡迎的飲料之一。它有很長的歷史。但是茶對每個人的意義不同。

In different countries people have different ideas about drinking tea. In China, for example, tea is always served when people get together. The Chinese drink it at any time of the day at home or in a teahouse. They like their tea with nothing else in it.

不同國家的人對於飲茶有不同的想法。像是在中國,當人們聚在一起的時候總會招待茶水。中國人隨時可以在家或在茶館裡喝茶。他們喜歡喝沒有加任何東西的茶。

Tea is very important in Japan. The Japanese have a special way of serving tea called a tea ceremony. Everything must be done in a special way in the ceremony. There is even a special room for it in a Japanese house.

茶在日本非常重要。日本人有一種特殊的上茶儀式叫做茶道。儀式中的每件事都必須以特殊的方式進行。日本的房子裡甚至有一個特別的房間用來喝茶。

Another tea-drinking country is England, and the late afternoon is called "teatime". Almost everyone has a cup of tea then. The English usually make tea in a teapot and drink it with cream, sugar and juice. They also eat cakes, cookies and little sandwiches at teatime.

另一個喝茶的國家是英國，下午還被稱為「喝茶時間」。那個時候幾乎每個人都會喝一杯茶。英國人常常把茶放在茶壺裡，飲用的時候配上奶精、糖和果汁。他們也在下午茶的時候吃蛋糕、餅乾和小型三明治。

19. Tea has a short history.（茶的歷史很短。）

    答案：(F 錯)

20. In China, people like to drink tea when they get together.

    （在中國，當人們聚在一起的時候喜歡喝茶。）

    答案：(T 對)

21. The Chinese only drink tea in the late afternoon.（中國人只在午後喝茶。）

    答案：(F 錯)

22. The Japanese have a special way of serving tea.（日本人有特殊的上茶方式。）

    答案：(T 對)

23. The English like their tea with nothing else in it.

    （英國人喜歡喝不加任呵東西的茶。）

    答案：(F 錯)

24. The passage talks about different cultures of drinking tea in four countries.

    （這段文章談到四個國家不同的喝茶文化。）

    答案：(F 錯)

V、Listen and fill in the blanks.（根據你所聽到的內容,用適當的單詞完成下面的句子。每空格限填一詞。）(6分)

Hello, my name is Jimmy. I'm a boy. I have something to tell you. I am fat and unhealthy. My mother is worried about my health. My favourite food is fried chicken, chocolate and ice cream. I don't like fruit or vegetables. At weekends, I only like watching TV at home. I hate doing exercise. Last week, I was ill. The doctor said I was not healthy because I had a bad diet. I will eat more fruit and vegetables and do more exercise. I think I will be thinner and healthier.

25. Jimmy's favourite food is <u>fried</u> chicken, chocolate and ice cream.
    Jimmy 最喜歡的食物是<u>炸雞</u>、巧克力和冰淇淋。

26. Jimmy's mother is worried about his health because he is fat and <u>unhealthy</u>.
    Jimmy 的媽媽很擔心他的健康因為他很胖也很<u>不健康</u>。

27. Jimmy hates doing <u>exercise</u> but he likes watching TV at weekends.
    Jimmy 痛恨做<u>運動</u>，但是他喜歡在周末看電視。

28. Last week, Jimmy was <u>ill</u>.
    上星期 Jimmy <u>生病</u>了。

29. Jimmy is not healthy because he has a bad <u>diet</u>.
    Jimmy 因為有不好的<u>飲食習慣</u>所以不健康。

30. Jimmy thinks he will be <u>thinner</u> and healthier.
    Jimmy 認為他將會<u>更瘦</u>、更健康。

全新英語聽力測驗原文及參考答案

Unit 7

Ⅰ、Listen and choose the right picture.（根據你所聽到的內容,選出相應的圖片。）
（6分）

1. Western people eat turkey on Thanksgiving Day.
   （西方人在感恩節的時候吃火雞。）

   答案：(A)

2. Our English teacher has taught us how to make some icy drinks by ourselves.
   （我們英文老師教過我們該怎麼自己做一些冰的飲料。）

   答案：(C)

3. David is used to eating Chinese food with chopsticks.
   （David 習慣用筷子吃中國食物。）

   答案：(F)

4. The Mid-autumn Festival is coming. My dad has bought some mooncakes.
   （中秋節快到了。我爸爸買了一些月餅。）

   答案：(B)

5. I'm going to buy some Italian food, for example, pizza.
（我要去買一些意大利食物，比如比薩。）

答案：(E)

6. Let's go to the McDonald's to have some hamburgers and French fries.
（我們去麥當勞吃漢堡和薯條吧。）

答案：(G)

II、Listen and choose the best response to the sentence you hear.（根據你所聽到的句子,選出最恰當的應答句。）（6分）

7. What about having a drink?（喝點東西怎麼樣？）
(A)That sounds great.（聽起來不錯。）
(B)I don't like any drinks.（我不喜歡任何飲料。）
(C)Let's have some drinks.（我們來喝點東西吧。）
(D)Drinks are good for us.（飲料對我們有好處。）

答案：(A)

8. What is the weather like today?（今天天氣如何？）
(A)It's November 1.（今天是十一月一日。）
(B)It's autumn.（現在是秋天。）
(C)It's windy and cold.（有點風也有點冷。）
(D)It's eight o'clock.（現在八點。）

答案：(C)

9. My mum prefers tea to coffee.（我媽媽寧可喝茶不喝咖啡。）
(A)So is my brother.（我弟弟也是。）
(B)Neither is my brother.（我弟弟也不是。）
(C)So does my brother.（我弟弟也是。）
(D)Neither does my brother.（我弟弟也不是。）

答案：(C)

10. What is the typical Japanese food?（典型的日本食物是什麼？）
(A)Hot dogs.（熱狗。）   (B)Raisin Scones.（葡萄乾鬆餅。）
(C)Sushi.（壽司。）   (D)Rice dumplings.（粽子。）

答案：(C)

11. Shall we hold a food festival to raise some money for the poor students?
（我們為貧困的學生舉辦一場美食展來籌募資金好嗎？）
(A)What a pity!（真可惜。）
(B)That's a great idea.（太棒了。）
(C)What is a food festival?（美食展是什麼？）
(D)We hold it at school.（我們在學校舉辦。）
答案：(B)

12. Can you show me the way to the nearest police station?
（你能告訴我去警察局最近的路線嗎？）
(A)I don't know.（我不知道。）
(B)The police station is over there.（警察局在那裡。）
(C)Walk for two blocks and then turn right.（走過兩個街口之後右轉。）
(D)The police station isn't far.（警察局不遠。）
答案：(C)

**III、Listen to the dialogue and choose the best answer to the question you hear.
（根據你所聽到的對話和問題,選出最恰當的答案。）（6分）**

13. W: When were you born?（W: 你什麼時候生的？）
M: I was born on June 30.（M: 我六月三十日生的。）
W: So you're one month older than I.（W: 這樣你就比我大一個月。）
Q: When was the girl born?（Q: 女孩什麼時候生的？）
(A)On June 13.（六月十三日。）　　　(B)On July 30.（七月三十日。）
(C)On June 30.（六月三十日。）　　　(D)On July 13.（七月十三日。）
答案：(B)

14. M: What festival do you like best, Lily?（M: Lily，妳最喜歡哪個節日？）
W: I like the Spring Festival best because I can get some red packets from my
parents.（W: 我最喜歡春節，因為爸媽會給我一些紅包。）
M: I like Mid-autumn Festival. I think the mooncakes are the most delicious
food in the world.（M: 我喜歡中秋節。我覺得月餅是世界上最好吃的食物。）
Q: What festival does Lily like best?（Q: Lily 最喜歡哪個節日？）
(A)The Spring Festival.（春節。）　　　(B)Mid-autumn Festival.（中秋節。）
(C)Lantern Festival.（元宵節。）　　　(D)Dragon Boat Festival.（端午節。）

答案：(A)

15. M: How do you keep in touch with your parents, Mary?
　　（M: Mary，妳如何跟妳的父母保持聯絡？）

　　W: I often talk with them on the phone. I call them twice a week.
　　（W: 我通常跟他們講電話。我一星期給他們打兩次電話。）

　　M: Why not talk with them on the computer? It's much cheaper.
　　（M: 為什麼不跟他們在電腦上聊天？那便宜多了。）

　　Q: How often does Mary call her parents?（Q: Mary 多久給她父母打一次電話？）
　　(A)Once a day.（一天一次。）　　　　　(B)Once a week.（一星期一次。）
　　(C)Twice a day.（一天兩次。）　　　　(D)Twice a week.（一星期兩次。）
　　答案：(D)

16. W: What present have you got for John, Eddie?
　　（W: Eddie，你要給 John 什麼禮物？）

　　M: A puppy. John likes dogs very much.（M: 一隻小狗。John 非常喜歡狗。）

　　W: Don't you know he likes hot dogs better?（W: 你不知道他更喜歡熱狗嗎？）

　　Q: What can we learn from the dialogue?
　　（Q: 我們可以從這段對話中知道些什麼？）
　　(A)John doesn't like hot dogs.（John 不喜歡熱狗。）
　　(B)John likes hot dogs.（John 喜歡熱狗。）
　　(C)The girl will give John a puppy.（女孩要給 John 一隻小狗。）
　　(D)Eddie will give John a hot dog.（Eddie 要給 John 一條熱狗。）
　　答案：(B)

17. W: How old is your father, Jack?（W: Jack，你父親幾歲？）

　　M: Oh, I'm fifteen now. My father is thirty-one years older than I.
　　（M: 喔，我現在十五歲。我父親比我大三十一歲。）

　　Q: How old is Jack's father?（Q: Jack 的父親幾歲？）
　　(A)Forty-two.（四十二歲。）　　　　　(B)Forty-six.（四十六歲。）
　　(C)Sixty-four.（六十四歲。）　　　　(D)Thirty-one.（三十一歲。）
　　答案：(B)

18. M: Tomorrow is Tree-planting Day. We'll go to plant trees on the beach.
　　（M: 明天是植樹節。我們要去海灘種樹。）

　　W: That's great.（W: 太棒了。）

　　Q: What season is it?（Q: 現在是什麼季節？）

(A)Spring.（春天。） (B)Summer.（夏天。）

(C)Autumn.（秋天。） (D)Winter.（冬天。）

答案：(A)

Ⅳ、**Listen to the dialogue and decide whether the following statements are True (T) or False (F).** （判斷下列句子內容是否符合你所聽到的對話內容,符合的用"T"表示,不符合的用"F"表示。）（6分）

Today is November 26th. It is Thanksgiving Day. The weather is fine. In the evening, Jenny and her mother went to her grandparents' home. When they got there, her cousin Tom was already there. Her grandmother was cooking a big turkey for them. Her grandfather was helping her grandmother in the kitchen. He was making some apple pies. When they saw Jenny, they gave her a big hug and laughed happily. Tom was playing with his toy horse. He was very happy when he saw Jenny. After one hour, they had a delicious dinner together. After the meal, Jenny and her mother went home. What a happy Thanksgiving Day today!

今天是十一月二十六日,感恩節。天氣很好。傍晚 Jenny 和她母親去祖父母家。當她們到了的時候,她的堂弟 Tom 已經在那兒了。她祖母正為他們煮一隻大火雞。她祖父在廚房幫她祖母的忙。他做了一些蘋果派。他們一看到 Jenny,就開心地笑着擁抱她。Tom 在玩他的玩具馬。他看到 Jenny 非常高興。一個小時後,他們一起享用美味的晚餐。用餐過後,Jenny 和她母親就回家了。今天真是一個快樂的感恩節啊!

---

19. Today is Thanksgiving Day. （今天是感恩節。）

答案：(T 對)

20. Jenny and her father went to her grandparents' home in the evening.
（傍晚 Jenny 和她父親去她祖父母家。）

答案：(F 錯)

21. Jenny's grandmother cooked a turkey for them. （Jenny 的祖母為他們煮了一隻火雞。）

答案：(T 對)

22. Jenny's grandmother made some apple pies. （Jenny 的祖母做了一些蘋果派。）

答案：(F 錯)

23. Tom was playing with his toy horse when Jenny saw him.

（Jenny 看到 Tom 的時候，Tom 正在玩他的玩具馬。）

答案：(T 對)

24. After the meal, Jenny and her father still stayed there.

（用餐過後，Jenny 和他父親仍然待在那兒。）

答案：(F 錯)

V、Listen and fill in the blanks.（根據你所聽到的內容,用適當的單詞完成下面的句子。每空格限填一詞。）（6分）

Japanese food is getting more and more popular. The most famous is sushi, which you can buy in the supermarkets all around the world. It's expensive to eat in the restaurants. You can save a lot of money by making it yourself. And it's easy. There are lots of different ways of making sushi. Here is one way.

日本食物越來越普遍。最有名的是壽司，你在世界各地的超級市場裡都可以買得到。在餐廳裡吃壽司很貴。自己做的話就可以省很多錢。而且作法很簡單。壽司有很多不同的作法。以下是其中一種做法。

1. Put some sugar, salt and vinegar in a cup.

1. 在杯子裡放一些糖、鹽和醋。

2. Boil some rice in two cups of water to make rice a little harder.

2. 用兩杯水煮米，這樣可以讓飯硬一點。

3. Put the rice into a large bowl. Add half a cup of vinegar.

3. 把飯放進一個大碗裡。加半杯醋。

4. Mix until the rice sticks together.

4. 混合攪拌直到飯黏在一起。

5. Make balls of rice. Each one should be about the size of a table tennis ball.

5. 做飯糰。每一個飯糰的大小差不多和桌球一樣大。

6. Cut the salmon into pieces, then press the salmon on top of the rice balls.

6. 把鮭魚切成片狀，然後把鮭魚壓在飯糰上。

7. Serve the sushi with green tea.

7. 以綠茶搭配著壽司來吃。

25. Japanese food is getting more and more <u>popular</u>.
日本食物越來越<u>普遍</u>。

26. The most <u>famous</u> Japanese food is sushi, which you can buy in the supermarkets all around the world.
<u>最有名的</u>日本食物是壽司，你在世界各地的超級市場裡都買得到它。

27. It's <u>expensive</u> to eat in the restaurants.
在餐廳裡吃壽司很<u>昂貴</u>。

28. You can save a lot of money by <u>making</u> it yourself. And it's easy. There are lots of different ways of making sushi. Here is one way.
自己<u>製作</u>的話就可以省很多錢。作法很簡單。壽司有許多不同的作法。以下是其中一種作法。

29. Put some <u>sugar</u>, salt and vinegar in a cup.
在一個杯子裡放一些<u>糖</u>、鹽和醋。

30. Cut the salmon into <u>pieces</u>, then press the salmon on top of the rice balls.
把鮭魚切成<u>片狀</u>，然後把鮭魚壓在飯糰上。

全新英語聽力測驗試題
Unit 8

I、Listen and choose the right picture.（根據你所聽到的內容,選出相應的圖片。）
（6分）

1. You mustn't throw rubbish on the ground.（你不可以把垃圾丟在地上。）
   答案：(G)

2. Peter's father works in a restaurant. He is a cook.
   （Peter 的父親在餐廳工作。他是一位廚師。）
   答案：(A)

3. The sign on the wall says "No smoking".（牆上的標示寫著:「禁止吸菸」。）
   答案：(F)

4. Little Kitty often helps her teacher carry books to the teachers' office.
   （小 Kitty 常常幫她的老師把書拿去教師辦公室。）
   答案：(B)

5. I have a new net-pal who is an American.（我有一個新網友,是美國人。）
   答案：(D)

6. My sister is good at playing the flute. （我姊姊擅長吹長笛。）

   答案：(C)

Ⅱ、Listen and choose the best response to the sentence you hear.（根據你所聽到的句子,選出最恰當的應答句。）（6分）

---

7. What can I do for you, sir?（先生，我能為你效勞嗎？）

   (A)Yes, I do.（是的，我做。）

   (B)All right.（好。）

   (C)I'd like a cup of coffee.（我想要一杯咖啡。）

   (D)No, you needn't.（不，你不需要。）

   答案：(C)

8. How do you go to school every day?（你每天怎麼去學校？）

   (A)By foot.（用腳。）

   (B)On foot.（步行。）

   (C)By my father's car.（搭我爸的車。）

   (D)On car.（在公車。）

   答案：(B)

9. Nice to meet you, Kitty.（Kitty 很高興認識你。）

   (A)You too.（你也是。）

   (B)Thank you.（謝謝你。）

   (C)Nice to meet you, too.（也很高興認識你。）

   (D)Hello.（哈囉。）

   答案：(C)

10. You've done a wonderful job.（你做得太棒了。）

    (A)Thanks.（謝謝。）　　　　　　　(B)No, it isn't.（不，它不是。）

    (C)Yes, I do.（是，我是。）　　　　(D)No problem.（沒問題。）

    答案：(A)

11. Which is more important, math or Chinese?（數學和中文那一個比較重要？）

    (A)Each.（每一個。）　　　　　　　(B)No, they aren't.（不，他們不重要。）

    (C)It's hard to say.（這很難說。）　(D)Yes, they are.（是的，它們是。）

    答案：(C)

12. My grandfather has got a bad cold.（我祖父感冒很嚴重。）

(A)He will be good.（他會是好的。）

(B)It's OK.（那還好。）

(C)I'm sorry to hear that.（我很抱歉聽到這件事。）

(D)That's great!（太棒了！）

答案：(C)

Ⅲ、Listen to the dialogue and choose the best answer to the question you hear.
（根據你所聽到的對話和問題,選出最恰當的答案。）（6分）

---

13. W: Which city do you like best?（W: 你最喜歡哪一個城市？）

M: I lived in Beijing when I was young. Now I live in Shanghai, but my favourite city is Hangzhou, so I hope to move there in the future.

（M: 年輕的時候我住在北京。我現在住在上海，但是我最喜歡的城市是杭州。所以我希望將來搬去那兒。）

Q: Which city does the man live in?（Q: 這個男人住在哪個城市？）

(A)Hangzhou.（杭州。）   (B)Shanghai.（上海。）

(C)Beijing.（北京。）   (D)Guangzhou.（廣州。）

答案：(B)

14. W: I can't find my suitcase.（W: 我找不到我的行李箱。）

M: You can go to the Lost and Found office. Maybe somebody found it.

（M: 你可以去失物招領處。或許有人發現它。）

W: OK. Where is it?（W: 好。在哪裡？）

M: Just over there, next to the bank.（M: 就在那兒，銀行的隔壁。）

Q: Where does the dialogue probably happen?（Q: 這段對話大概在哪裡發生？）

(A)In a bank.（在銀行。）   (B)At a restaurant.（在餐廳。）

(C)In an office.（在辦公室。）   (D)At the airport.（在機場。）

答案：(D)

15. W: The mooncakes with nuts in them are very delicious. Please have a taste of them.（W: 有堅果的月餅非常好吃。請嚐嚐看。）

M: Oh, no, thanks. I can't have any more.（M: 不用了，謝謝。我再也吃不下了。）

Q: Why doesn't the man want to eat the mooncakes?

（Q: 這個男人為什麼不想吃月餅？）

(A)They are not delicious.（它們不好吃。）

(B)He is hungry.（他餓了。）

(C)He is full.（他飽了。）

(D)He doesn't like mooncakes.（他不喜歡月餅。）

答案：(C)

16. W: What day is it today?（W: 今天星期幾？）

M: It's Wednesday. When are we going to visit Jinmao Building?

（M: 今天星期三。我們甚麼時候去參觀金茂大樓？）

W: Oh, we're going to visit it the day after tomorrow.（W: 喔，我們後天去參觀。）

M: I think we'll have a good time there.（M: 我想我們在那裡會很開心。）

Q: When are they going to visit Jinmao Building?

（Q: 他們甚麼時候去參觀金茂大樓？）

(A)Two days later.（兩天後。）　　　　(B)Tomorrow.（明天。）

(C)Wednesday.（星期三。）　　　　(D)Monday.（星期一。）

答案：(A)

17. W: Hello, Tom. You look tired today.（W: 哈囉，Tom。你今天看起來很累。）

M: Yes. I went to bed too late last night.（M: 是的。我昨天晚上太晚睡了。）

W: You'd better go to bed earlier this evening.（W: 你今天晚上最好早點睡。）

M: But tomorrow we will have an exam. I'll do some revision.

（M: 但是明天我們有一場考試。我要復習。）

W: If you don't have enough rest, you won't do well in the exam.

（W: 如果你休息得不夠，你會考不好的。）

Q: What is the girl's suggestion to Tom?（Q: 女孩給了 Tom 甚麼建議？）

(A)Do some revision.（復習。）　　　　(B)Have a good rest.（好好休息。）

(C)Go to bed late.（晚點睡。）　　　　(D)Do well in English.（讀好英文。）

答案：(B)

18. W: I was born in 1982. What about you?（W: 我一九八二年生。你呢？）

M: I was born in 1983. My sister is two years younger than me.

（M: 我一九八三年生。我妹妹比我小兩歲。）

W: Do you go to the same school?（W: 你們去同樣的學校嗎？）

M: Yes. But we are not in the same class.（M: 是的。但是我們在不同班級。）

Q: The girl is younger than the boy, isn't she?（Q: 女孩比男孩年輕，是嗎？）

(A)No, she isn't.（不，她不是。）　　　　(B)No, she is.（不，她是。）

(C)Yes, she is. （是，她是。） (D)Yes, she isn't. （是，她不是。）

答案：(A)

IV、Listen to the dialogue and decide whether the following statements are True (T) or False (F). （判斷下列句子內容是否符合你所聽到的對話內容,符合的用"T"表示,不符合的用"F"表示。）（6分）

New Zealand is a country in Australia. It lies in the south part of the world. There is an old story in New Zealand. It says that the God separated his parents, the Sky and the Earth, to create the world we live in. This story was brought to the World Expo 2010 by the New Zealand Pavilion under the theme "Cities of Nature: Living between Land and Sky". The pavilion has an area of 2,000 square metres. It has three parts: the welcoming space, the interior, and the roof garden.

紐西蘭是在澳洲大陸的一個國家。它位於南半球。紐西蘭有一個古老的故事。故事描述上帝隔離了袖的父母，天空與陸地，來創造我們所居住的世界。這個故事是由紐西蘭展示館，在「自然城市：生活在陸地與天空之間」的主題下，向二零一零年世界博覽會所提出的。這個展示館佔地兩千平方公尺。它分為三個部分：歡迎區、內展區，以及屋頂花園。

The welcoming space was in front of the pavilion. There were many young people who could speak Chinese well in the welcoming space at the Expo. They introduced the culture and history of New Zealand to the visitors. When people entered the pavilion, they could experience a day in a New Zealand city starting from the sea, through the suburbs, the city centre and the mountains.

歡迎區在展示館的前方。世博會的歡迎區有非常多會說中文的年輕人。他們向參觀者介紹紐西蘭的文化和歷史。當人們進入展示館時，他們可以從海洋開始、到郊區、市中心與山區，來體驗紐西蘭城市的一天 。

---

19. New Zealand is in South America.（紐西蘭在南美洲。）

    答案：(F 錯)

20. The old story in New Zealand says the God's parents created the world we live in. （紐西蘭的古老故事描述了上帝的父母創造了我們所居住的世界。）

    答案：(F 錯)

21. The theme of the New Zealand Pavilion is "Better city, better life".

（紐西蘭展示館的主題是「更好的城市、更好的生活」。）

答案：(F 錯)

22. The pavilion has an area of 2,000 square meters.（展示館佔地兩千平方公尺。）

答案：(T 對)

23. There are four parts in the New Zealand Pavilion.（紐西蘭展示館有四個部分。）

答案：(F 錯)

24. When people entered the pavilion, they could experience a day in a New Zealand city.（當人們進入展示館時，他們可以體驗紐西蘭城市的一天。）

答案：(T 對)

V、Listen and fill in the blanks.（根據你所聽到的內容,用適當的單詞完成下面的句子。每空格限填一詞。）（6分）

Many people ask me the question: When is the best time to visit Shanghai? Usually, I couldn't give an answer. However, these days, when I walk on Nanjing Road or visit the Bund at night, I regret that I didn't tell my friends that September may be the best time to visit Shanghai. Why? Because the Shanghai Travel Festival starts in September every year.

許多人問我這個問題：甚麼時候遊覽上海是最好的時間？通常我不給答案。但是，當我這幾天晚上去南京路或外灘走走的時候，我很後悔我沒告訴我的朋友，九月可能是遊覽上海最好的時間。為什麼呢？因為上海旅遊節每年九月展開。

There are many activities during the festival. It lasts for about three weeks. There are carnivals, boat shows on the Huangpu River, International Firework Show, F1 Race, Beer Festival, Germany Week and so on. There are also many other international events during the three weeks in Shanghai.

在旅遊節的期間有非常多活動。歷時約三個星期。有嘉年華會、黃浦江上的船隻表演、國際煙火秀，FI賽車，啤酒節，德國週…等等。在那個三星期裡，上海也有許多其他國際性的活動。

During the Travel Festival, all the lights will be turned on. The whole city is so beautiful. I believe that 50％ of the beauty of Shanghai is its lights.

在旅遊節期間，所有的燈光都點亮了。整個城市是如此的美麗。我相信上海百分之五十的美就是來自它的燈光。

Also, it is cooling down and sunny. The weather is great. The lights are great. September should be the best time to visit Shanghai!

還有，天氣涼爽而且晴朗。天氣很棒。燈光很棒。九月應該就是遊覽上海最好的時間！

25. Usually, I couldn't give an <u>answer</u> when people ask me the question: when is the best time to visit Shanghai?

當有人問我這個問題：甚麼時候是遊覽上海最好的時間？我通常不給<u>答案</u>。

26. <u>September</u> may be the best time to visit Shanghai.

<u>九月</u>或許就是遊覽上海最好的時間。

27. There are many <u>activities</u> during the Shanghai Travel <u>festival</u>.

在上海旅遊<u>節</u>的期間有非常多<u>活動</u>。

28. There are also many other <u>international</u> events during the three weeks in Shanghai.

在那三個星期中，上海也有許多其他<u>國際性</u>的活動。

29. I believe that <u>50%</u> of the beauty of Shanghai is its lights.

我相信上海<u>百分之百分之五十</u>的美就是來自它的燈光。

全新英語聽力測驗原文及參考答案

Unit 9

Ⅰ、Listen and choose the right picture. (根據你所聽到的內容,選出相應的圖片。)
（6分）

A   B   C

D   E   F   G

1. I have watched a film about a pleasant goat named Xiyangyang.
   （我看過一部關於一隻快樂小羊的影片，叫做喜洋洋。）
   答案：(A)

2. Have you seen a cartoon about a lovely mouse and a cunning cat?
   （你看過一部卡通是關於一隻可愛的老鼠和一隻狡猾的貓嗎？）
   答案：(C)

3. The four children are singing in the music room. （四個孩子在音樂教室唱歌。）
   答案：(B)

4. Snow White is my favourite cartoon character.（白雪公主是我最喜歡的卡通角色。）
   答案：(G)

5. Kingkong is a kind gorilla which saves a beautiful girl from danger.
   （金剛是一隻和善的大猩猩，它把漂亮的女孩從危險中解救出來。）

答案：(F)

6. Jay had a concert and sang many songs by himself.
    （Jay 有一場演唱會，唱了許多他自己寫的歌曲。）

    答案：(E)

II、Listen and choose the best response to the sentence you hear.（根據你所聽到的句子,選出最恰當的應答句。）（6分）

7. Which film is your favourite film about adventure?
    （與探險有關的電影你最喜歡哪一部？）
    (A)The Adventures of Tom Sawyer.（湯姆歷險記。）
    (B)The Snow White.（白雪公主。）
    (C)The Swan Lake.（天鵝湖。）
    (D)The Happy Clown.（快樂的小丑。）

    答案：(A)

8. How long does the film last?（這部電影歷時多久？）
    (A)For two and a half hours.（兩個半小時。）
    (B)In two and a half hours.（在兩個半小時以內。）
    (C)The film is about love.（這是關於愛情的電影。）
    (D)What is the film about?（這部電影與甚麼有關？）

    答案：(A)

9. I'd rather watch some documentaries.（我寧願看記錄片。）
    (A)So do I.（我也是。）　　　　(B)Neither do I.（我也不是。）
    (C)So would I.（我也是。）　　　(D)Neither would I.（我也不是。）

    答案：(C)

10. What are the rules at home?（家裡的規矩是甚麼？）
    (A)We must keep our bedroom clean.（我們必須保持臥室整潔。）
    (B)We must walk on the zebra lines.（我們必須走斑馬線。）
    (C)We mustn't eat or drink here.（我們不可以在這裡飲食。）
    (D)We must obey the traffic rules.（我們必須遵守交通規則。）

    答案：(A)

11. It's late. I must go home now. （很晚了。我現在必須回家。）
    (A)Yes, I will. （好，我會。）
    (B)It isn't late. （現在不晚。）
    (C)Take care on your way home. （回家要小心。）
    (D)With pleasure. （我的榮幸。）
    答案：(C)

12. Shall I pick you up tomorrow morning? （我明天早上來接你好嗎？）
    (A)Never mind. （別介意。）
    (B)It doesn't matter. （沒關係。）
    (C)Thanks. It's kind of you. （謝謝。你真好。）
    (D)Yes, I'd love to. （好，我很想。）
    答案：(C)

Ⅲ、Listen to the dialogue and choose the best answer to the question you hear.
（根據你所聽到的對話和問題,選出最恰當的答案。）（6分）

---

13. M: I'd like to have a look at those shoes in the window, please.
    （M: 麻煩妳，我想看一看櫥窗裡的那些鞋子。）
    W: Yes. What size do you take? （W: 好的。你要甚麼尺寸？）
    Q: Where does the dialogue probably take place?（Q: 這段對話大概在哪裡發生？）
    (A)In a shoe shop. （在鞋店。）　　　(B)At a supermarket. （在超級市場。）
    (C)In a hotel. （在旅館。）　　　(D)In a glass factory. （在玻璃工廠。）
    答案：(A)

14. W: I don't know how to use the computer. Can you show me, Tom?
    （W: 我不知道該怎麼用這台電腦。Tom，你可以教我嗎？）
    M: Well, I don't know, either. Maybe Jim can help.
    （M: 喔，我也不知道。Jim 也許能幫忙。）
    Q: What does the woman want to do? （Q: 那個女人想做甚麼？）
    (A)Operate the computer. （操作電腦。）
    (B)Show Tom. （展示 Tom。）
    (C)Help Jim. （幫助 Jim。）
    (D)Look for the computer. （找電腦。）
    答案：(A)

15. W: What time is it now, Jim?（W: Jim，現在幾點？）

M: It's ten o'clock.（M: 十點。）

W: Have you finished your homework yet?（W: 你的功課寫完了嗎？）

M: Yes. I finished it half an hour ago.（M: 是的。我半小時以前就寫完了。）

Q: When did Jim finish his homework?（Q: Jim 甚麼時候寫完功課？）

(A)At 9:30.（九點三十分。） (B)At 10.（十點。）

(C)At 10:30.（十點三十分。） (D)At 11.（十一點。）

答案：(A)

16. M: Stop walking, Kitty. The red light is on!（M: Kitty，別走了。紅燈亮了！）

W: But there are no cars or buses here.（W: 但是這裡沒有汽車或公車。）

M: We must obey the traffic rules.（M: 我們必須遵守交通規則。）

Q: Where are they talking?（Q: 他們在哪裡說話？）

(A)In a car.（在車裡。） (B)At the crossing.（在斑馬線上。）

(C)On a bus.（在公車上。） (D)At home.（在家裡。）

答案：(B)

17. M: Is your home on the second floor, Lucy?（M: Lucy, 妳家在二樓嗎？）

W: Yes, Tom.（W: 是的，Tom。）

M: Oh, my home is three floors higher than yours.

   （M: 喔，我家比你家高三層樓。）

Q: Which floor does Tom live on?（Q: Tom 住在幾樓？）

(A)On the 1st floor.（一樓。） (B)On the 2nd floor.（二樓。）

(C)On the 5th floor.（五樓。） (D)On the 6th floor.（六樓。）

答案：(C)

18. W: What are you doing, John?（W: John，你在做甚麼？）

M: I am watching a film called Lion King. It is one of my favourite films.

   （M: 我在看一部叫做獅子王的電影。這是我最喜歡的電影之一。）

W: You like watching cartoons? Don't you think they're childish?

   （W: 你喜歡看卡通？你不覺得那很孩子氣嗎？）

M: No, not at all. I think cartoons are more interesting than other movies. They

   are full of love and fun.

   （M: 一點也不。我覺得卡通比其它電影更有趣。他們充滿了愛與樂趣。）

Q: What kind of films does the man like best?

   （Q: 那個男人最喜歡哪一種電影？）

(A)Cartoons.（卡通。） (B)Love stories.（愛情故事。）

(C)Adventures.（探險片。） (D)Horror films.（恐怖片。）

答案：(A)

IV、Listen to the dialogue and decide whether the following statements are True (T) or False (F).（判斷下列句子內容是否符合你所聽到的對話內容,符合的用"T"表示,不符合的用"F"表示。）（6分）

The old name for films was moving pictures. In America they still call them "movies" and they say "Shall we go to the movies?" when we say "Shall we go to the cinema?"

電影(film)的舊名是「移動式相片」。美國人稱它們為"movie"。當我們說「Shall we go to the cinema?（我們去看電影好嗎？）」的時候，美國人說：「Shall we go to the movies?」

A boy once said to his friend, "Do you like moving pictures?" The friend thought that he was going to be invited to the cinema, so he said, "Yes, please. I like moving pictures very much."

曾經有一個男孩對他的朋友說：「你喜歡移動式相片嗎？」那個朋友認為他要邀請他去看電影，所以他說：「是的。我非常喜歡移動式相片。」

"Good!" said the first boy. "My father has a picture shop. He sells pictures. This evening I have to move fifty heavy boxes of pictures from one room to another. You like moving pictures so I'm sure you will enjoy moving these pictures for me."

「太棒了！」第一個男孩說。「我爸爸有一間相片商店。他賣相片。今天晚上我要從一個房間搬五十箱很重的相片到另一間房間。你喜歡移動相片，我相信你會很樂意幫我搬這些相片。」

---

19. Movies are also called moving pictures.（電影也被稱為移動式相片）

答案：(T 對)

20. The boy's father sold pictures.（男孩的爸爸賣相片。）

答案：(T 對)

21. The boy had to move fifty boxes of pictures from one room into another.

（男孩必須從一個房間搬五十箱相片到另一個房間。）

答案：(T 對)

22. His friend was very pleased to help the boy move pictures.
（他的朋友非常樂意幫他搬相片。）
答案：(F 錯)

23. At last, they saw an interesting film. （最後，他們看了場有趣的電影。）
答案：(F 錯)

24. In fact, the boy's friend liked watching films. （事實上，男孩的朋友喜歡看電影。）
答案： (T 對)

Ⅴ、Listen and fill in the blanks. （根據你所聽到的內容,用適當的單詞完成下面的句子。每空格限填一詞。）（6分）

I like seeing films very much. I see films every week. Last week, I saw a film called After Shocks. It's a film about a disaster. I saw it in Shanghai Movie Center at 6:30 p.m. The cinema was crowded with people. The film tells a story about a terrible earthquake happened in Tangshan in 1976. The film talks about human love and asks us to cherish our lives every day. Though it lasted for more than two hours, it was great and I was moved to tears. When I went out of the cinema, it was nearly 9:30 p.m. I really had a good time that night.

我非常喜歡電影。我每個星期都看電影。上星期我看了一部叫做 After Shocks（唐山大地震）的電影。這是一部災難片。我下午六點半在上海電影中心看的。電影院擠滿了人。這部電影是講述一九七六年發生在唐山的可怕地震。電影談到人間有情，並要我們珍惜每天的生活。雖然它長達兩個多小時，但是非常棒，而且我也感動落淚。當我走出電影院的時候，已經將近晚上九點三十分。那天晚上我真的過得很愉快。

---

25. I saw a film called After Shocks in Shanghai Movie <u>Center</u> at 6:30 p.m. last week.
上星期，我下午六點半去上海電影中心看了一部電影，叫做 After Shocks。

26. The film tells a story about a <u>terrible</u> earthquake happened in Tangshan in 1976.
這部電影講述一九七六年發生在唐山的可怕地震。

27. The film talks about human love and asks us to <u>cherish</u> our lives every day.
這部電影談到人間有情，並要我們珍惜每天的生活。

28. The film lasted for more than <u>two</u> hours.
這部電影片長超過<u>兩</u>小時。

29. I was <u>moved</u> to tears.
我<u>感動</u>落淚。

30. When I went out of the cinema, it was nearly <u>9:30</u> p.m.
當我離開電影院的時候，已經將近晚上<u>九點三十分</u>了。

全新英語聽力測驗原文及參考答案

Unit 10

I、Listen and choose the right picture.（根據你所聽到的內容,選出相應的圖片。）（6分）

1. My little brother's birthday is coming. I'm going to buy him a toy bear.
（我弟弟的生日快到了。我要買一個泰迪熊給他。）
答案：(A)

2. Mr. Lin bought a new sofa for his new flat.
（Lin 先生為他的新公寓買了一套新沙發。）
答案：(D)

3. Peter has sent his daughter a new dress.（Peter 送了一件新洋裝給他的女兒。）
答案：(E)

4. It's convenient for us to wear T-shirts in summer.
（夏天穿 T 恤對我們來說很方便。）
答案：(C)

5. If you want to buy a school bag, you can go to the stationery store.
（如果你想買書包，你可以去文具店。）

    答案：(G)

6. You can buy a watch on the fourth floor.（你可以到四樓買手錶。）

    答案：(B)

II、Listen and choose the best response to the sentence you hear.（根據你所聽到的句子,選出最恰當的應答句。）（6分）

---

7. What size do you wear?（你穿幾號？）
    (A)Shirts.（襯衫。）   (B)Sports shoes.（運動鞋。）
    (C)Size medium.（中號。）   (D)Clothes.（服裝。）

    答案：(C)

8. Can I have a look at that pair of jeans?（我可以看看那條牛仔褲嗎？）
    (A)No, you can't.（不，你不可以。）
    (B)The jeans are over there.（牛仔褲在那邊。）
    (C)Sure.（當然可以。）
    (D)I don't like the color.（我不喜歡這個顏色。）

    答案：(C)

9. I'm terribly sorry to bother you.（很抱歉打擾到你 。）
    (A)It doesn't matter.（沒關係。）   (B)No, you don't.（不，你沒打擾。）
    (C)Yes, you do.（是的，你打擾了。）   (D)Don't bother me.（別打擾我。）

    答案：(A)

10. We're going to have a ball. Would you like to join us?
    （我們要辦一個舞會。你想參加嗎？）
    (A)What's the matter?（怎麼了？）
    (B)Sure. What time?（當然。幾點？）
    (C)Yes, I do.（是的，我願意。）
    (D)The ball will be at my place.（舞會將會在我住的地方。）

    答案：(B)

11. I prefer jeans with blue belts to the ones with yellow belts.
    （比起配上黃色腰帶的，我比較喜歡配上藍色腰帶的牛仔褲。）

(A)So do I.（我也是。）   (B)So I do.（我這麼做的。）

(C)Neither do I.（我也不是。）   (D)Neither I do.（我也不這麼做。）

答案：(A)

12. What is the duration of that film?（那部電影歷時多久？）

    (A)Three hours.（三小時。）   (B)In three hours.（在三小時以內。）

    (C)At three o'clock.（在三點。）   (D)Since three hours.（自三小時開始。）

答案：(A)

Ⅲ、Listen to the dialogue and choose the best answer to the question you hear. （根據你所聽到的對話和問題,選出最恰當的答案。）（6分）

---

13. W: Can I help you?（W: 我能為你服務嗎？）

    M: Yes. I bought this pair of shoes here yesterday. I like the style, but can you change them for white ones? I don't like black ones.

    （M: 是的。我昨天在這裡買了這雙鞋。我喜歡這個樣式,但是你能換成白色的嗎？我不喜歡黑色的。）

    Q: Why does the man want to change the shoes?（Q: 那個男人為什麼想換鞋？）

    (A)He doesn't like the style.（他不喜歡那個樣式。）

    (B)He doesn't like the colour.（他不喜歡那個顏色。）

    (C)The size is too big.（尺寸太大。）

    (D)The size is too small.（尺寸太小。）

    答案：(B)

14. M: How much are the tomatoes?（M: 番茄多少錢？）

    W: They are four yuan a kilo.（W: 一公斤四元。）

    M: I'll take two kilos, please.（M: 請給我兩公斤。）

    Q: How much should the man pay for the tomatoes?

    （Q: 那個男人要花多少錢買番茄？）

    (A)4 yuan.（四元。）   (B)8 yuan.（八元。）

    (C)12 yuan.（十二元。）   (D)14 yuan.（十四元。）

    答案：(B)

15. M: Lucy, you look really cool in the glasses.（M: Lucy,妳戴眼鏡看起來好酷。）

    W: Thank you. I think Nancy also looks nice in that hat.

    （W: 謝謝你。我覺得 Nancy 戴那頂帽子也很好看。）

M: So she does.（M: 沒錯。）

Q: What does Lucy wear?（Q: Lucy 戴甚麼？）

(A)A hat.（帽子。）　　　　　　　　(B)Bracelet.（手鐲。）

(C)Earrings.（耳環。）　　　　　　(D)Glasses.（眼鏡。）

答案：(D)

16. M: How long have you studied in this school?（M: 你在這所學校念了多久？）

　　W: For three years. And I'll study for another three years.（W: 有三年了。我還要再念三年。）

　　Q: How long should the girl study in her school altogether?

　　　（Q: 女孩在她的學校唸書一共要多久時間？）

　　(A)For three years.（三年。）　　　(B)For four years.（四年。）

　　(C)For five years.（五年。）　　　(D)For six years.（六年。）

　　答案：(D)

17. W: How nice your shoes are! How much did you pay for them?

　　　（W: 你的鞋子真好看。你花多少錢買的？）

　　M: 15 dollars.（M: 十五元。）

　　W: I like them very much. How much must I pay for a pair of women's shoes?

　　　（W: 我非常喜歡。我買一雙女鞋要花多少錢呢？）

　　M: 5 dollars more.（M: 再多五元。）

　　Q: How much is a pair of women's shoes?（Q: 女鞋一雙多少錢？）

　　(A)10 dollars.（十元。）　　　　(B)15 dollars.（十五元。）

　　(C)20 dollars.（二十元。）　　　(D)25 dollars.（二十五元。）

　　答案：(C)

18. W: Can I help you, sir?（W: 先生，我能為你服務嗎？）

　　M: Yes. I need a sweater.（M: 是的。我需要一件毛衣。）

　　W: What about this black one?（W: 這件黑色的怎麼樣？）

　　M: Do you have it in size large?（M: 你有大號尺寸的嗎？）

　　W: Of course.（W: 當然有。）

　　Q: Where are they now?（Q: 他們現在在哪裡？）

　　(A)At a clothes shop.（在服裝店。）　(B)In a restaurant.（在餐廳。）

　　(C)At an office.（在辦公室。）　　(D)In the fire station.（在消防局。）

　　答案：(A)

Lin Miaoke, a nine-year-old Beijing girl, has become one of the biggest stars after the 2008 Beijing Olympic Opening Ceremony. Lin Miaoke sang the song "A Hymn to My Motherland" at the opening ceremony of Beijing Olympic Games. Her sweet smile and beautiful voice touched almost everyone who was watching the opening ceremony.

林妙可，一名九歲大的北京女孩，在二零零八北京奧運開幕式之後變成了大明星。林妙可在北京奧運開幕式上唱了一首叫做「A Hymn to My Motherland(歌唱祖國)」的歌曲。她甜美的笑容與優美的嗓音幾乎感動了觀賞開幕式的每一個人。

The nine-year-old girl is now studying at West Street Primary School in Dongchun District, Beijing. Besides singing, she also likes folk dancing, playing the piano and flute. She first came in a television advertisement with actress Zhao Wei at the age of six. In 2007, she appeared in a TV advertisement with Olympic champion Liu Xiang and an advertisement for the Beijing Olympics.

這名九歲大的女孩現在在北京東城區的西街小學念書。除了唱歌以外，她也喜歡跳土風舞、彈鋼琴和吹長笛。她六歲的時候第一次與女明星趙薇演出電視廣告。二零零七年，她與奧運冠軍劉翔在北京奧運的廣告上一起出現。

The famous director Zhang Yimou chose her among thousands of children in Beijing. Lin Miaoke is very famous now. Now we can see her pictures on many newspapers and magazines.

知名導演張藝謀從北京上千名兒童中挑選了她。林妙可現在非常有名。我們可以在許多報章雜誌上看到她的相片。

19. Lin Miaoke became famous after the 2008 Beijing Olympic Games.
（林妙可在二零零八北京奧運之後成名。）

答案：(T 對)

20. Lin Miaoke sang the song "A Hymn to My motherland" at the opening ceremony. （林妙可在開幕式上唱了一首歌叫做「A Hymn to My motherland」。）

答案：(T 對)

21. She likes playing the piano and flute, but she can't dance.
（她喜歡彈鋼琴和吹長笛，但是她不跳舞。）
答案：（F 錯）

22. She was six years old when she appeared in the TV advertisement with Liu Xiang. （當她與劉翔一起出現在電視廣告上的時候，她六歲大。）
答案：（F 錯）

23. The director Zhang Yimou chose her among all the children in Shanghai.
（導演張藝謀從上海所有的兒童中挑選了她。）
答案：（F 錯）

24. Now we can see her photos on many newspapers and magazines.
（現在我們可以在許多報章雜誌上看到她的相片。）
答案：（T 對）

V、Listen and fill in the blanks.（根據你所聽到的內容,用適當的單詞完成下面的句子。每空格限填一詞。）（6分）

M: Good morning. What can I do for you, lady?（M: 早安。小姐，我能為妳效勞嗎？）

W: I want to buy a pair of sports shoes of size 8. （W: 我想買一雙尺寸八號的鞋子。）

M: What about the black pair? It's 200 dollars.
（M: 那雙黑色的怎麼樣？那雙兩百元。）

W: It's smart but too expensive. Can you show me another pair?
（W: 很時髦但是太貴了。你能介紹其他雙鞋子嗎？）

M: The white pair is nice. Will you try them on?
（W: 這雙白色的不錯。你要不要試試看？）

W: Yes, they fit me very well. How much then? （W: 它非常適合我。要多少錢？）

M: 50 dollars cheaper. （M: 便宜五十元。）

W: All right. I'll take them. By the way, how much is the T-shirt with stripes?
（W: 好。我買了。另外，條紋 T 恤多少錢？）

M: The one with red stripes is 80 dollars, and the one with blue stripes is 40 dollars.（M: 紅色條紋的八十元，藍色條紋的四十元。）

W: I'll take the red one. （W: 我要紅色的。）

M: OK. So you want a pair of white sports shoes and a T-shirt with red stripes.
（M: 好。所以你要一雙白色運動鞋和一件紅條紋 T 恤。）

W: Yes. Here is the money. （W: 是的。錢在這裡。）

25. The woman wants to buy a pair of <u>sports</u> shoes.
那個女人要買一雙<u>運動</u>鞋。

26. The <u>black</u> pair is 200 dollars.
<u>黑色</u>的那一雙要價兩百元。

27. The white pair <u>fits</u> the woman well.
白色的那一雙很<u>適合</u>那個女人。

28. The white pair is <u>150</u> dollars.
白色的那一雙要<u>一百五十</u>元。

29. The woman likes the T-shirt with red <u>stripes</u>.
那個女人喜歡有紅色<u>條紋</u>的 T 恤。

30. The woman will pay <u>230</u> dollars for them.
那個女人要花<u>兩百三十</u>元。

全新英語聽力測驗原文及參考答案

Unit 11

Ⅰ、Listen and choose the right picture.（根據你所聽到的內容,選出相應的圖片。）（6分）

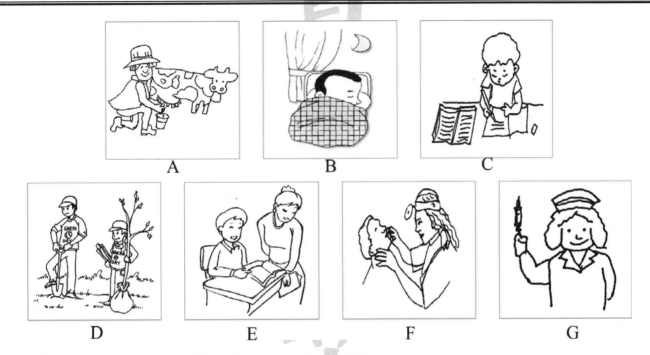

7. The nurse works in No.6 People's Hospital.
（那位護士在第六人民醫院工作。）

答案：(G)

8. The farmer is milking the cow on his farm.
（農夫在他的農場裡擠牛奶。）

答案：(A)

9. Jack sleeps early every evening and he never stays up late.
（Jack 每天晚上很早睡，他從不熬夜。）

答案：(B)

10. Miss Zhang is my Chinese teacher. She is a nice and patient lady.
（Zhang 小姐是我的中文老師。她是一位和藹可親也很有耐心的小姐。）

答案：(E)

11. Yesterday was the Earth Day. Our class planted trees in the park.
（昨天是地球日。我們班在公園種樹。）

答案：(D)

12. John went to the dentist's to have his bad teeth pulled out.
（John 去看牙醫，要把他的壞牙齒給拔掉。）

答案：(F)

II、Listen and choose the best response to the sentence you hear.（根據你所聽到的句子,選出最恰當的應答句。）（6分）

---

13. How often do you go to the library?（你多久去一次圖書館？）
(A)To the library.（去圖書館。）　　(B)This Sunday.（這個星期天。）
(C)At 3 o'clock.（在三點。）　　(D)Once a week.（一星期一次。）

答案：(D)

14. The Japanese sushi is very delicious.（日本壽司非常好吃。）
(A)I'm glad you like it.（我很高興你喜歡。）
(B)It's good.（那很好。）
(C)Yes, it is.（是的，它是。）
(D)I'm sorry to hear that.（我很抱歉聽到那件事。）

答案：(A)

15. You'd better eat less sweet food.（你最好少吃甜食。）
(A)That's all right.（沒關係。）
(B)You are welcome.（不客氣。）
(C)Thank you for your advice.（感謝你的忠告。）
(D)No, I won't.（不，我不要。）

答案：(C)

16. What's wrong with you?（你怎麼了？）
(A)I have got a bad cold.（我重感冒。）
(B)I will go to the park tomorrow.（我明天要去公園。）
(C)I am doing my homework.（我在做功課。）
(D)There is something wrong with me.（我有點不大對勁。）

答案：(A)

17. I can't play the guitar.（我不會彈吉他。）
    (A)So can I.（我也會）　　　　　　　　(B)Neither can I.（我也不會。）
    (C)So can't I.（我也不會。）　　　　　　(D)Neither can't I.（我也不是不會。）
    答案：(B)

18. How is your brother?（你的哥哥還好嗎？）
    (A)Much better. Thank you.（好多了。謝謝你。）
    (B)I'm better. Thanks.（我比較好。謝謝。）
    (C)He's writing a report.（他在寫報告。）
    (D)You are so kind.（你真好。）
    答案：(A)

Ⅲ、Listen to the dialogue and choose the best answer to the question you hear.
（根據你所聽到的對話和問題,選出最恰當的答案。）（6分）

---

19. W: Boys, let's have a 100m running test. Are you ready?
    （W: 男孩們，我們來進行一百公尺跑步測驗。準備好了嗎？）
    M: Mrs. Wang, my legs were hurt this morning because of a small accident.
    （M: Wang 老師，今天早上一場小車禍使我的腿受傷了。）
    W: Really? Do you want to go to the clinic?（W: 真的嗎？你要去診所嗎？）
    Q: Where does the dialogue probably take place?
    （Q: 這段對話大概發生在甚麼地方？）
    (A)At the cinema.（在電影院。）
    (B)On the school playground.（在學校操場。）
    (C)At the clinic.（在診所。）
    (D)In the hospital.（在醫院。）
    答案：(B)

20. M: What's your plan after you finish school, Betty?
    （M: Betty,畢業後妳有甚麼計劃？）
    W: Well, my parents want me to be a teacher, but I'd prefer to be a reporter.
    （W: 嗯，我父母要我當老師，但是我更喜歡當記者。）
    Q: What does Betty want to be after she finishes school?
    （Q: 畢業以後 Betty 想當甚麼？）
    (A)A teacher.（老師。）　　　　　　　(B)A reporter.（記者。）

(C)A doctor.（醫生。）   (D)A scientist.（科學家。）

答案：(B)

21. W: What time will the play begin tonight?（W: 今晚表演幾點開始？）

    M: It'll begin at eight. When shall we start?

    （M: 八點開始。我們該甚麼時後出發呢？）

    W: 7 o'clock, OK?（W: 七點好嗎？）

    M: The traffic is very heavy at 7. Let's leave half an hour earlier.

    （M: 七點交通繁忙。我們提早半小時離開吧。）

    Q: When will they leave for the theatre?（Q: 他們幾點前往戲劇院？）

(A)At 6.（六點。）   (B)At 7.（七點。）

(C)At 6:30.（六點三十分。）   (D)At 7:30.（七點三十分。）

答案：(C)

22. W: I'm so glad it's sunny today. The rain has finally stopped.

    （W: 我好高興今天是晴天。雨終於停了。）

    M: I hope it will be fine tomorrow, too. We will have a picnic.

    （M: 我希望明天天氣也一樣好。我們要去野餐。）

    W: But the weather report says it's going to rain again tomorrow.

    （W: 但是氣象報告說明天又要下雨了。）

    Q: What's the weather going to be like tomorrow?

    （Q: 明天的天氣怎麼樣？）

(A)It will be rainy.（會下雨。）   (B)It will be cloudy.（會是陰天。）

(C)It will be snowy.（會下雪。）   (D)It will be windy.（會有風。）

答案：(A)

23. M: Lily, can you help me with my math?（M: Lily，妳能在數學上幫幫我嗎？）

    W: Peter, I would like to. But I'm afraid I am not good at math, either. Tom always gets full marks in math. Let's ask him for help.

    （W: Peter, 我很想。但是恐怕我的數學也不怎麼樣。Tom 的數學一直拿滿分。我們去找他幫忙吧。）

    Q: Who is good at math?（Q: 誰擅長於數學？）

(A)Lily.   (B)Peter.   (C)Tom.   (D)Jack.

答案：(C)

24. W: Good morning, Dad. What's for breakfast? （W：爸，早安。早餐吃甚麼？）

M: I've prepared milk, noodles and some bread.

（M：我準備了牛奶、麵、和一些麵包。）

Q: What hasn't Dad prepared? （Q：爸爸沒有準備甚麼？）

(A)Milk. （牛奶。） (B)Bread. （麵包。）

(C)Pizza. （披薩。） (D)Noodles. （麵。）

答案：(C)

Ⅳ、**Listen to the dialogue and decide whether the following statements are True (T) or False (F).** （判斷下列句子內容是否符合你所聽到的對話內容,符合的用"T"表示,不符合的用"F"表示。）（6分）

Jimmy is a model student at school. He is good at all his subjects except math. But he never gives it up. He always does a lot of math problems. His math teacher also helps him. I think he will be good at math soon. Kitty is a model student, too. She lives far away from school, but she is never late for school. It takes her about 50 minutes to get to school. First, she takes the underground. Then, she takes the bus. Tom is not a model student. He doesn't finish homework on time. In class, he often talks with others. He often fails in exams. Last week, his little brother asked him a very easy question, but he didn't know the answer. Tom felt very sad. He decided to work hard from then on.

Jimmy 在學校是一位模範生。除了數學以外,他所有的科目都很擅長。但是他從不放棄。他一直做很多數學習題。他的數學老師也協助他。我想他的數學很快就會進步。Kitty 也是模範生。她住的離學校很遠,但是她上學從不遲到。她要花五十分鐘去上學。她先搭地鐵。然後再搭公車。Tom 不是模範生。他不準時完成功課。他在班上常常和其他人說話。他考試常常不及格。上個星期,他的弟弟問他一個非常簡單的問題,但是他答不出來。Tom 覺得很難過。從那時候開始他決定努力用功。

---

25. Jimmy is good at all his subjects. （Jimmy 擅長所有科目。）

答案：(F 錯)

26. Jimmy always does a lot of math problems. （Jimmy 一直做很多數學習題。）

答案：(T 對)

27. It takes Kitty about 40 minutes to get to school. （Kitty 要花四十分鐘去上學。）

答案：(F 錯)

28. Kitty takes a bus first and then she takes the underground.
（Kitty 先搭公車，再搭地鐵。）

答案：(F 錯)

29. Tom couldn't answer his brother's question.（Tom 不能回答他弟弟的問題。）

答案：(T 對)

30. Tom is a model student now.（Tom 現在是模範生。）

答案：(F 錯)

V、Listen and fill in the blanks.（根據你所聽到的內容,用適當的單詞完成下面的句子。每空格限填一詞。）(6分)

Dear Alice,

12 <u>September</u> is my birthday. I'd like to <u>invite</u> you to my birthday party. The party will <u>begin</u> at 6 p.m. at my flat. Many of our friends are coming. We are going to have a <u>barbecue</u> in the garden. We are also going to sing karaoke. We'll watch <u>cartoons</u>, too. I hope you will be <u>free</u> that day. See you then.

Yours,

Jenny

親愛的 Alice，

<u>九月</u>十二日是我的生日。我想<u>邀請</u>你來參加我的生日派對。派對會在我的公寓舉辦，晚上六點<u>開始</u>。我們許多朋友都會來。我們要在花園<u>烤肉</u>。我們也要唱卡拉ＯＫ。我們還要看<u>卡</u>通。我希望你那天<u>有</u>空。到時候見。

你的好朋友

Jenny

全新英語聽力測驗原文及參考答案

Unit 12

Ⅰ、Listen and choose the right picture.（根據你所聽到的內容,選出相應的圖片。）
（6分）

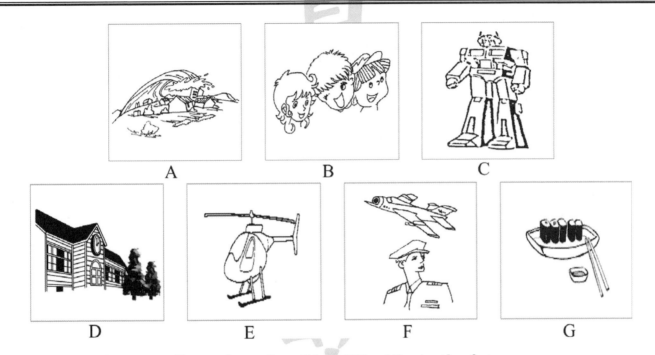

1. The children are discussing what life will be like in the future.
   （孩子們在討論未來的生活會是如何。）

   答案：(B)

2. Perhaps people will be able to go to work by helicopter in 50 years' time.
   （在五十年間內，人們或許可以搭直升機上班。）

   答案：(E)

3. I think robots will be very useful in our life in the future.
   （我認為機器人在我們未來的生活中將會非常有用。）

   答案：(C)

4. My ambition is to be a pilot in the future.
   （我未來的志向是要當一名飛機駕駛。）

   答案：(F)

5. Sushi is a kind of famous food in Japan. （壽司在日本是一種知名的食物。）

    答案：(G)

6. A flood flew away some villages in western part of China last month.

    （上個月洪水流經中國西半部的一些村落。）

    答案：(A)

II、Listen and choose the best response to the sentence you hear.（根據你所聽到的句子,選出最恰當的應答句。）（6分）

7. I think perhaps people will be able to live on the Mars.

    （我認為人們將有可能住在火星上。）

    (A)I think not. （我認為不是。）

    (B)I think so, too. （我也這麼認為。）

    (C)Yes, I do. （是的，我認為。）

    (D)So will we. （我們也會。）

    答案：(B)

8. Give me two kilos of tomatoes, please. （請給我兩公斤番茄。）

    (A)How much are the tomatoes? （番茄多少錢？）

    (B)OK. Ten yuan, please. （好。一共十元。）

    (C)The tomatoes are fresh. （番茄很新鮮。）

    (D)At the market. （在市場。）

    答案：(B)

9. Sorry, I have broken your window, Mr. White.

    （White 先生，對不起，我打破你的窗戶了。）

    (A)You are welcome. （不客氣。）

    (B)Never mind. Take care next time. （別介意。下次小心一點。）

    (C)All right. （好的。）

    (D)Here you are. （給你。）

    答案：(B)

10. What will you say when you invite a friend to a party?

    （當你邀請朋友來參加派對的時候你會說甚麼？）

    (A)Would you like to come to my party? （你想來我的派對嗎？）

(B)Come to my party.（來我的派對。）

(C)My party is great.（我的派對很棒。）

(D)You must come to my party.（你一定要來我的派對。）

答案：(A)

11. What day is it today?（今天星期幾？）

　　(A)In the morning.（在早上。）　　　　(B)In Japan.（在日本。）

　　(C)In April.（在四月。）　　　　　　(D)It is Sunday.（今天星期天。）

　　答案：(D)

12. Can you help me wash the dishes?（你可以幫我洗碗嗎？）

　　(A)Yes, I can.（是的，我能。）　　　　(B)No, I can't.（不，我不能。）

　　(C)With pleasure.（我很樂意。）　　　(D)Thank you.（謝謝你。）

　　答案：(C)

Ⅲ、Listen to the dialogue and choose the best answer to the question you hear.
（根據你所聽到的對話和問題,選出最恰當的答案。）（6分）

---

13. W: What kind of film do you like?（W: 你喜歡哪一種電影？）

　　M: I used to like funny films very much. But now I like action films.
　　　（M: 我以前非常喜歡搞笑片。但是我現在喜歡動作片。）

　　W: That sounds good! Who is your favourite film star?
　　　（W: 聽起來不錯！誰是你最喜歡的電影明星？）

　　M: I like Jacky Cheng best.（M: 我最喜歡成龍。）

　　Q: What kind of film does the boy like now?（Q: 男孩現在喜歡哪一種電影？）

　　(A)Action films.（動作片。）

　　(B)Funny films.（搞笑片。）

　　(C)Documentaries.（紀錄片。）

　　(D)Love stories.（愛情片。）

　　答案：(A)

14. W: Excuse me, how much is the red dress?（W: 抱歉，這件紅色洋裝多少錢？）

　　M: It's 150 yuan.（M: 一百五十元。）

　　W: What about the white shirt?（W: 這件白色襯衫呢？）

　　M: 120 yuan.（M: 一百二十元。）

　　W: OK! I will take both.（W: 好。我兩件都買。）

Q: How much is the woman going to pay?（Q: 這個女人要付多少錢？）

(A)120 yuan.（一百二十元。）　　　(B)150 yuan.（一百五十元。）

(C)270 yuan.（兩百七十元。）　　　(D)300 yuan.（三百元。）

答案：(C)

15. M: It's too far away to go on foot. I think you should take a bus.

（M: 走路去實在太遠了。我認為你該搭公車。）

W: But waiting for buses takes lots of time. I'd like to borrow a bike.

（W: 但是等公車要花好多時間。我想借腳踏車。）

Q: How will the woman go?（Q: 這個女人要怎麼去？）

(A)On foot.（走路。）　　　　　(B)By bike.（騎腳踏車。）

(C)By bus.（搭公車。）　　　　(D)By taxi.（搭計程車。）

答案：(B)

16. M: Where can we go tomorrow, Mary?（M: Mary，我們明天可以去哪兒呢？）

W: We can go to Nanjing Road to do some shopping.

（W: 我們可以去南京路逛街買東西。）

M: You know men hate shopping. What about going to Dongping National Forest
Park?（M: 你知道的，男人最討厭購物。去東平國家森林公園怎麼樣？）

W: It's too far. I suggest we go to Shanghai Zoo or Changfeng Park.

（W: 太遠了。我建議我們去上海動物園或是長風公園。）

M: I don't like animals, but I like boating.（M: 我不喜歡動物，但是我喜歡划船。）

Q: Where will they possibly go?（Q: 他們大概會去哪裡？）

(A)Shanghai Zoo.（上海動物園。）

(B)Dongping National Forest Park.（東平國家森林公園。）

(C)Changfeng Park.（長風公園。）

(D)Nanjing Road.（南京路。）

答案：(C)

17. M: What a sunny day, Alice!（M: Alice，今天天氣真好啊！）

W: Yes, it is! Shall we go out for a walk?（W: 對啊！我們去散步好不好？）

M: That's a good idea.（M: 那真是好主意。）

W: Right. I think spring will come soon.（W: 是的。我想春天就快來了。）

Q: What season is it now?（Q: 現在是甚麼季節？）

(A)Spring.（春天。）　　　　　(B)Summer.（夏天。）

(C)Autumn.（秋天。）　　　　　(D)Winter.（冬天。）

答案：(D)

18. M: You look so pretty in this green dress with white spots.
    （M: 妳穿這件有白色點點的綠色洋裝真好看。）
    W: Thank you. In fact, yellow is my favourite, but the shop assistant said there were no yellow dresses at that time.
    （W: 謝謝。實際上我最喜歡黃色，但是那時候店員說沒有黃色洋裝了。）
    Q: What color is the woman's favourite colour?
    （Q: 這個女人最喜歡的顏色是甚麼顏色？）
    (A)Green.（綠色。）   (B)Yellow.（黃色。）
    (C)Blue.（藍色。）   (D)Black.（黑色。）
    答案：(B)

IV、Listen to the dialogue and decide whether the following statements are True (T) or False (F).（判斷下列句子內容是否符合你所聽到的對話內容,符合的用"T"表示,不符合的用"F"表示。）（6分）

In the year 2050, there will be different kinds of materials for clothes. Special chemicals will make the clothes keep clean—they will never get dirty. They will help us save water and money.

到 2050 年，衣物將有不同種類的材質。特殊的化學物質將使衣物保持乾淨——它們永遠不會髒。它們將使我們既省水又省錢。

We won't worry about what to wear to go to school every day. Children won't go to school. They will stay at home in front of their computers. Children can wear their favourite clothes. It will be fun.

我們將不用擔心每天要穿什麼上學了。孩子們將不去學校。他們會待在家裡的電腦前。孩子們可以穿他們最喜歡的衣服。這將會很有趣。

What do you think? Do you think it will be fun? What do you think school clothes and school life will be like in 2050?

你覺得怎麼樣呢？你覺得這樣有趣嗎？到了 2050 年，你覺得校服和學校生活會是怎樣呢？

---

19. In the year 2015, there will be different kinds of materials for clothes.
    （到了 2015 年，衣物將有不同種類的材質。）
    答案：(F 錯)

20. The special clothes will easily get dirty.（特殊的衣物將很容易變髒。）

　　答案：(F 錯)

21. Because of the special clothes, we will save water and money.

　　（因為有了特殊的衣物，我們將省水又省錢。）

　　答案：(T 對)

22. Children need to wear uniforms at school every day in 2050.

　　（到了 2050 年，孩子們每天都要穿制服去學校。）

　　答案：(F 錯)

23. Children will stay at home and learn things by computer.

　　（孩子們將在家裡透過電腦來學習。）

　　答案：(T 對)

24. According to the writer, children will be able to design their favorite clothes.

　　（根據作者的說法，孩子們將可以設計他們喜歡的衣服。）

　　答案：(F 錯)

Ⅴ、Listen and fill in the blanks.（根據你所聽到的內容,用適當的單詞完成下面的句子。每空格限填一詞。）（6 分）

M: Why are you looking so disappointed, Tina?

M: Tina，妳怎麼看起來有點失望的樣子？

W: I have just seen the film The Day After Tomorrow. It is a disaster film. The temperature in some parts of the world will keep dropping. And there will be heavy snowstorm and floods everywhere. People will keep shivering.

W: 我剛剛看了「明日過後」這部電影。這是一部災難片。氣溫在世界某些地方會持續下降。到處都有強烈暴風雪和水災。人們一直在發抖。

M: Oh, my God! It's awful. But perhaps things won't be so bad as you think. Although there is terrible air pollution, I think we will be able to solve the problem. For example, plant more trees and drive less cars. Perhaps we can move to another planet by spacecraft. Perhaps we can live in cities under the sea.

M: 天啊！真可怕。但也許事情不是你想的那麼糟。雖然有嚴重的空氣汙染，但我認為我們將有可能解決這個問題。譬如：多種樹，少開車。也許我們可以搭乘太空船移居到另一個星球。也許我們可以住在海底的城市。

W: Maybe you are right, Mike. Let's do something to protect the earth from now on.

W: Mike，你也許是對的。就讓我們從現在開始做些保護地球的事吧。

25. Tina looks <u>disappointed</u>.
   Tina 看起來很<u>失望</u>。

26. The <u>temperature</u> in some parts of the world will keep dropping.
   <u>氣溫</u>在世界某些地方會持續下降。

27. And there will be heavy snowstorm and floods <u>everywhere</u>.
   <u>每個地方</u>都有嚴重的暴風雪和水災。

28. Although there is terrible air <u>pollution</u>, Mike thinks we can solve the problem.
   雖然空氣<u>汙染</u>很嚴重，但是 Mike 認為我們可以解決這個問題。

29. Perhaps we can move to another <u>planet</u> by spacecraft.
   也許我們可以搭太空船移居到另一個<u>星球</u>。

30. Let's do something to <u>protect</u> the earth from now on.
   讓我們從現在起就來做些<u>保護</u>地球的事吧。

全新英語聽力測驗試題
Unit 13

A   B   C

D   E   F   G

1. On Christmas Day little children hope to get presents from Santa Claus.
    （小朋友希望在聖誕節得到聖誕老人的禮物。）
    答案：(G)

2. I'd like to buy a sweater with spots.（我想買一件有點點花紋的毛衣）
    答案：(E)

3. John managed to paint the walls himself at home.
    （John 計畫在家裡自己油漆牆壁。）
    答案：(F)

4. The wind blows fiercely and the leaves start falling from the tree. Autumn is
    coming.（風猛烈地吹，葉子開始從樹上掉落。秋天就要來了。）
    答案：(B)

5. The air pollution is getting more and more serious in some developing countries.

（空氣汙染在某些開發中國家變得越來越嚴重了。）

答案：(D)

6. We watched the final of the FIFA World Cup 2010 excitedly at home.
（我們在家興奮地觀看二零一零年世界杯足球賽的總決賽。）

答案：(C)

Ⅱ、Listen and choose the best response to the sentence you hear. （根據你所聽到的句子,選出最恰當的應答句。）（6分）

7. My ambition is to be an architect. （我的志向是當一名建築師。）
(A)So do mine. （我的也是。）　　　(B)Neither do mine. （我的也不是。）
(C)So is mine. （我的也是。）　　　(D)Neither is mine. （我的也不是。）

答案：(C)

8. Could you turn down the radio a bit? （你把收音機轉小聲一點好嗎？）
(A)Yes, I can. （是的，我可以。）
(B)No, I can't. （不，我不可以。）
(C)I'm sorry to have bothered you. （很抱歉打擾到你了。）
(D)Yes, I could. （是的，我可以。）

答案：(C)

9. May I speak to Mr. Brown? （請 Brown 先生聽電話好嗎？）
(A)Yes, I am. （是的，我是。）　　　(B)Yes, he is. （是，他是。）
(C)Yes, speaking. （我就是。）　　(D)I'm Mr. Brown. （我是 Brown 先生。）

答案：(C)

10. Many trees fell down in the typhoon last week.
（許多樹在上星期的颱風中傾倒了。）
(A)What a pity! （好可惜。）　　　(B)What fun! （好有趣！）
(C)I know. （我知道。）　　　　　(D)I don't think so. （我不這麼認為。）

答案：(A)

11. Could you leave a message? （請你留言好嗎？）
(A)Certainly. （當然。）　　　　　(B)That's all right. （沒關係。）
(C)That's right. （對的。）　　　　(D)You're welcome. （不客氣。）

答案：(A)

12.　How often do you brush your teeth every day?（你每天刷幾次牙？）

　　(A)In a day.（一天內。）　　　　　(B)Twice a day.（一天兩次。）

　　(C)At 7 o'clock.（七點。）　　　　(D)For two times.（兩次。）

　　答案：(B)

Ⅲ、Listen to the dialogue and choose the best answer to the question you hear.
（根據你所聽到的對話和問題,選出最恰當的答案。）（6分）

13.　W: Can I help you, sir?（W: 先生，我能為你服務嗎？）

　　M: Sure. Is your library open on Saturday?（M: 嗯。你們的圖書館星期天開放嗎？）

　　W: No. It's open from Monday to Friday. We don't work at the weekend.

　　　（W: 不開放。星期一到星期五開放。我們周末不上班。）

　　Q: When can people borrow books from the library?

　　　（Q: 人們甚麼時候可以到圖書館借書？）

　　(A)At the weekend.（周末。）　　　(B)On weekdays.（平日。）

　　(C)On Saturday.（星期六。）　　　(D)On Sunday.（星期天。）

　　答案：(B)

14.　W: May I speak to John, please?（W: 請找 John 聽電話好嗎？）

　　M: Sorry, you've got the wrong number.（M: 抱歉，你打錯號碼了。）

　　W: Is that 6627594?（W: 是 6627594 嗎？）

　　M: No. It's 6624594.（M: 不。這裡是 6624594。）

　　Q: What's John's telephone number?（Q: John 的電話號碼是幾號？）

　　(A)6624594.　　　　(B)6627594.　　　　(C)6627495.　　　　(D)6624495.

　　答案：(B)

15.　W: How lovely you were! How old were you then?

　　　（W: 你真可愛！那時候你幾歲？）

　　M: I was three years old. My aunt took the photo. She likes children very much.

　　　（M: 我三歲。我阿姨拍的相片。她非常喜歡小孩。）

　　Q: What are they doing?（Q: 他們在做甚麼？）

　　(A)They are looking at the photo.（他們在看相片。）

　　(B)They are visiting a kindergarten.（他們在參觀幼稚園。）

　　(C)They are talking to an aunt.（她們在跟一位阿姨說話。）

　　(D)They are watching TV.（他們在看電視。）

答案：(A)

16. W: Peter, what can we use water for?（W: Peter，我們可以拿水來做甚麼？）

    M: Sorry, Miss Wu, I'm not quite sure.)（M: Wu 小姐，很抱歉，我不大確定。）

    W: You'd better work harder. Sit down, please. Who can help Peter?
      （W: 你最好努力一點。請坐下。誰能來幫 Peter？）

    Q: What is Miss Wu?（Q: Wu 小姐是做甚麼的？）

    (A)A student.（學生。）　　　　　　　　　(B)A nurse.（護士。）

    (C)A teacher.（老師。）　　　　　　　　(D)A doctor.（醫生。）

    答案：(C)

17. W: When will our plane leave?（W: 我們的飛機何時離開？）

    M: At 10:45 tomorrow morning. But we have to arrive at the airport two hours
      earlier.（M: 明天早上十點四十五分。但是我們要提早兩小時到機場。）

    Q: When must they get to the airport?（Q: 他們必須何時抵達機場？）

    (A)10:45.（十點四十五分。）　　　　　(B)9:45.（九點四十五分。）

    (C)11:45.（十一點四十五分。）　　　(D)8:45.（八點四十五分。）

    答案：(D)

18. W: Do you want me to get you anything? I'm leaving now.
      （W: 你要我幫你買東西嗎？我現在要走了。）

    M: I want three loaves of bread and two kilos of apples.
      （M: 我要三條麵包和兩公斤蘋果。）

    W: Okay. I will get them.（W: 好。我會去買。）

    Q: Where is the girl going?（Q: 女孩要去哪裡？）

    (A)To a post office.（郵局。）　　　　(B)To a food shop.（食品店。）

    (C)To a library.（圖書館。）　　　　　(D)To a bank.（銀行。）

    答案：(B)

Ⅳ、Listen to the dialogue and decide whether the following statements are
True (T) or False (F). （判斷下列句子內容是否符合你所聽到的對話內容,符合的
用"T"表示,不符合的用"F"表示。）（6分）

　　Forests are very important to men and animals. They provide food and
shelters for animals. If there are no trees, animals will have no food or shelters.
They will soon die. We get many materials from forests. We get food from trees.

Wood is useful for making paper and furniture. Land is also important. We use oil to make plastic. We use metal to make cans and use clay for making bowls and plates. We get sand from beaches. We use sand to make glass. All the things we get from forests and land are necessary in our daily life. We can't live without forests or land. Everyone should protect forests and our environment.

森林對人類和動物來說非常重要。森林為動物提供了食物和藏匿之處。如果沒有了樹木，動物將沒有食物和藏匿之處。牠們很快就會死亡。我們從森林取得很多素材。我們從樹木中取得食物。木材可以用來製作紙張和家具。陸地也很重要。我們利用石油來製作塑膠。用金屬來製作罐頭，用黏土來製作碗盤。我們從海灘取得沙子。我們利用沙子來做玻璃。我們從森林與陸地取得的所有東西，在我們的日常生活中都是必要的。沒有了森林或陸地我們將不能生存。每個人都應該保護森林與我們的環境。

---

19. Forests are important to us. （森林對我們很重要。）

答案：(T 對)

20. Trees only provide food for animals. （樹木只能為動物提供食物。）

答案：(F 錯)

21. Animals will die quickly without trees. （沒有了樹木，動物很快就會死亡 。）

答案：(T 對)

22. Cans are made of clay. （罐頭是黏土做的。）

答案：(F 錯)

23. Glass is made from sand on the beaches. （玻璃是由海灘的沙所製成的。）

答案：(T 對)

24. Everything we use in our daily life comes from trees and land.
（我們日常生活中所使用的每一件東西都來自樹木和陸地。）

答案：(F 錯)

V、Listen and fill in the blanks.（根據你所聽到的內容,用適當的單詞完成下面的句子。每空格限填一詞。）（6分）

M: Hello, Lingling, you look so sad and worried.
（M: 哈囉 Lingling，妳看起來很難過、很擔心的樣子。）

W: Yes. I think all of us feel sad these days because of the mudslide from the mountain in early August, in Gansu.

（W: 是的。這幾天我們大家都因為八月上旬在甘肅山區發生的土石流而感到難過。）

M: Yes, it was terrible. Many people were hurt. About 1,300 people died.

（M: 是的，那真的很可怕。許多人受傷了。大約一千三百人死亡。）

W: Many children lost their parents, and many parents lost their children. Most of them lost their homes. Students there can't go to school.

（W: 許多孩子失去了父母，許多父母失去了孩子。他們大部分都失去了家園。學生們沒辦法上學。）

M: This is the worst news of the year. But what can we do to help them?

（M: 這是今年最糟的消息。然而，我們能做些甚麼來幫助他們呢？）

W: Just now we had a class meeting. We've decided to raise some money for them. We are going to buy some books, schoolbags, pens, rulers and something else for them. （W: 就在剛才我們開了一次班級會議。我們決定為他們募捐。我們要買書、書包、筆、尺和其他物品給他們。）

M: That's great. My dad is an architect. He is going to help the people to rebuild their homes. （M:太棒了。我爸爸是建築師。他要幫助他們重建家園。）

W: I hope everything will go well with them. （W: 我希望他們能事事順利。）

M: I hope so, too. （M: 我也這麼希望。）

25. The mudslide happened in early <u>August</u> in Gansu.
    甘肅的土石流發生在<u>八月</u>上旬。

26. Many people were <u>hurt</u>.
    許多人<u>受傷</u>。

27. About <u>1,300</u> people died.
    大約<u>一千三百</u>人死亡。

28. We had a class <u>meeting</u> just now.
    我們剛才有個班級<u>會議</u>。

29. We've decided to <u>raise</u> some money for them.
    我們決定為他們<u>募捐</u>。

30. The boy's father is an <u>architect</u>.
    男孩的父親是<u>建築師</u>。

全新英語聽力測驗原文及參考答案
Unit 14

I、Listen and choose the right picture.（根據你所聽到的內容,選出相應的圖片。）
（6分）

1. We went to Sanya to enjoy the sea view this summer holiday.
   （這個暑假我們去三亞欣賞海景。）

   答案：(G)

2. When autumn comes, leaves start falling from the trees.
   （當秋天來臨的時候，樹葉開始從樹上掉落。）

   答案：(F)

3. Thunder storms always happen in summer in Shanghai.
   （在上海，雷雨總是在夏天發生。）

   答案：(D)

4. Look! The little boy is making a snowman happily in the park.
   （看啊！那個小男孩在公園裡快樂的堆雪人呢。）

   答案：(B)

5. In spring, it's fun to fly kites in the open area.
（春天的時候，在空曠的區域放風箏很有趣。）

答案：(C)

6. The wind begins blowing hard.（風開始猛烈的吹。）

答案：(A)

II、Listen and choose the best response to the sentence you hear.（根據你所聽到的句子,選出最恰當的應答句。）（6分）

---

7. May I speak to Jenny?（我能找 Jenny 說話嗎？）
   (A)I'm Jenny.（我是 Jenny。）
   (B)Yes, I am.（是的，我是。）
   (C)Sorry, she isn't here.（抱歉，她不在。）
   (D)Who are you?（你是誰？）

   答案：(C)

8. How are you and your parents?（你和你的父母都好嗎？）
   (A)We are friends.（我們是朋友。）
   (B)We are fine. Thanks.（我們很好，謝謝。）
   (C)We have been to Japan.（我們去了日本。）
   (D)We will stay at home.（我們會待在家。）

   答案：(B)

9. What time will you come back?（你什麼時候回來？）
   (A)After three days.（三天之後。）   (B)At midnight.（午夜。）
   (C)Three days later.（晚三天。）   (D)Since three days.（自三天前。）

   答案：(B)

10. You look upset. Is anything wrong?（你看起來很沮喪。有甚麼問題嗎？）
    (A)I've lost my key rings.（我掉了我的鑰匙。）
    (B)I'm 15 years old.（我十五歲。）
    (C)I will buy a new shirt.（我要買一件新襯衫。）
    (D)I am right.（我是對的。）

    答案：(A)

11. How much is the ticket?（票價多少？）
   (A)To Beijing.（到北京。）
   (B)100 yuan.（一百元。）
   (C)At five in the afternoon.（在下午五點。）
   (D)It's for sale.（拍賣中。）
   答案：(B)

12. Robin, this is my mother. Mum, this is my friend, Robin.
   （Robin, 這位是我母親。媽，這是我的朋友 Robin。）
   (A)Bye bye.（再見。）
   (B)Hello. Nice to meet you.（哈囉，很高興認識你。）
   (C)What's your name?（你的大名是？）
   (D)Who's your friend?（你的朋友是誰？）
   答案：(B)

Ⅲ、Listen to the dialogue and choose the best answer to the question you hear.
（根據你所聽到的對話和問題,選出最恰當的答案。）（6分）

13. W: Has the train left?（W: 火車離開了嗎？）
   M: No, it is leaving in ten minutes. And it's three forty now.
      （M: 還沒，它十分鐘後離開。現在是三點四十分。）
   Q: When is the train leaving?（Q: 火車何時離開？）
   (A)3:30.（三點三十分。）   (B)3:40.（三點四十分。）
   (C)3:50.（三點五十分。）   (D)4:00.（四點。）
   答案：(C)

14. W: What does winter make you think of?（W: 冬天讓你想起甚麼？）
   M: Winter makes me think of snow. What about you?
      （M: 冬天讓我想起下雪。妳呢？）
   W: Winter makes me think of skating.（W: 冬天讓我想起滑雪。）
   Q: What does winter make the girl think of?（Q: 冬天讓女孩想起甚麼？）
   (A)Snow.（下雪。）   (B)Skating.（滑雪。）
   (C)Coldness.（寒冷。）   (D)Warm clothes.（溫暖的衣服。）
   答案：(B)

15. M: What can I do for you?（M: 我能為妳效勞嗎？）

W: I'd like to buy three tickets. How much does one ticket cost?

（W: 我要買三張票。一張票多少錢？）

M: Forty yuan for an adult. Twenty yuan for a child.

（M: 成人票一張四十元。兒童票一張二十元。）

W: I need a ticket for an adult and two tickets for children.

（W: 我要一張成人票，兩張兒童票。）

Q: How much is the woman going to pay for the tickets altogether?

（Q: 那個女人一共要花多少錢買票？）

(A)80 yuan.（八十元。）　　　　　　　(B)100 yuan.（一百元。）

(C)60 yuan.（六十元。）　　　　　　　(D)120 yuan.（一百二十元。）

答案：(A)

16. M: Can I take these books home, please?（M: 我可以把這幾本書帶回家嗎？）

W: Yes, here you are. You can keep them for two weeks.

（W: 好的。給你。你可以保留兩個星期。）

Q: Who is the man talking to?（Q: 那個男人在對誰說話？）

(A)A shop assistant.（店員。）　　　　(B)A book seller.（書商。）

(C)A librarian.（圖書管理員。）　　　　(D)A secretary.（秘書。）

答案：(C)

17. W: What's the weather like today, John?（W: John，今天天氣怎麼樣？）

M: It's cloudy and late afternoon it will rain. But the weather report says it's going to be a fine day tomorrow.

（M: 陰天，下午就會下雨了。但是氣象報告說明天天氣不錯。）

W: Really? What about going for a picnic tomorrow?

（W: 真的嗎？明天去野餐怎麼樣？）

M: That's a great idea.（M: 這真是個好主意。）

Q: What will the weather be like tomorrow?（Q: 明天天氣如何？）

(A)Rainy.（有雨。）　　　　　　　　　(B)Stormy.（暴風雨。）

(C)Foggy.（有霧。）　　　　　　　　　(D)Sunny.（晴朗。）

答案：(D)

18. W: Dad, listen! There is big noise outside. What happens?

（W: 爸，你聽！外面有好大的噪音。發生甚麼事了？）

M: Oh! Some children are setting off firecrackers.（M: 喔！有些孩子在放鞭炮。）

W: Why do they do so?（W: 他們為什麼要這麼做？）

M: In China, it's fun for children to set off firecrackers, visit relatives and receive red packets during the Spring Festival.

　　（M: 在中國的春節期間，放鞭炮、拜訪親戚、拿紅包，對孩子們來說很有趣。）

Q: What don't children do during the Spring Festival?

　　（Q: 春節期間孩子們不做甚麼？）

(A)To eat mooncakes. （吃月餅。）　　　(B)To set off firecrackers. （放鞭炮。）

(C)To receive red packets. （拿紅包。） (D)To visit relatives. （拜訪親戚。）

答案：(A)

IV、Listen to the dialogue and decide whether the following statements are True (T) or False (F). （判斷下列句子內容是否符合你所聽到的對話內容,符合的用"T"表示,不符合的用"F"表示。）（6分）

Plants 植物

We can see many plants around us every day. There are over 300,000 species of plants in the world. They play an important part in our life. Now let's see the importance of plants.

我們每天都可以在周遭看到許多植物。世界上有超過三十萬種植物。它們在我們的生活中扮演重要的角色。現在讓我們來看看植物的重要性。

Plants bring natural beauty to us. Many people like decorating their rooms with flowers or other plants. The plants in the room can make people feel comfortable and relaxed.

植物為我們帶來自然美景。許多人喜歡利用花朵或其他植物來裝飾他們的房間。房間裡的植物可以讓人們感到舒適與放鬆。

Of course, plants can do more things for people. They help people clean the air we breathe and they are just like little oxygen factories. They also help hold the soil and stop soil and water from moving away.

當然，植物可以為人們做更多事。植物有助於清潔我們呼吸的空氣，它們就像小型的氧氣工廠。它們也能抓住土壤，不讓土壤與水分流失。

Both people and animals can get food from plants. People and animals can't live without plants. Plants are useful. Workers can make furniture out of wood, clothes out of cotton, and so on. Some plants can also be used as medicine.

人和動物可以從植物中獲得食物。沒有了植物，人和動物將無法生存。植物很有用。工人可以做木製家具、棉製衣服...等等。有些植物還可以做成藥物。

Plants are really important and we should protect them and make good use of them.

植物真的很重要，我們應該要保護它們並且好好的利用它們。

19. There are more than thirty million kinds of plants in the world.
（世界上有超過三千萬種植物。）

答案：(F 錯)

20. People like decorating rooms with flowers and other plants.
（人們喜歡用花和其他植物來裝飾房間。）

答案：(T 對)

21. People and animals only get food from plants.（人和動物只從植物來獲得食物。）

答案：(F 錯)

22. Unlike animals, people can't live without plants.
（人不像動物，沒有了植物就無法生存。）

答案：(F 錯)

23. People can make clothes out of cotton.（人們可以做出棉製的衣服。）

答案：(T 對)

24. All medicines are made from plants.（所有的藥物都是從植物製造的。）

答案：(F 錯)

Ⅴ、Listen and fill in the blanks.（根據你所聽到的內容,用適當的單詞完成下面的句子。每空格限填一詞。）（6分）

Almost everybody likes to play. All over the world, men and women, boys and girls enjoy sports. Sports help to keep people healthy and let them live happily.

幾乎每一個人都喜歡遊玩。全世界的男人、女人、男孩、女孩都喜歡運動。運動有助於人們維持健康，活得快樂。

Sports change with the seasons. People play different games in winter and summer. Sailing is fun in warm weather, while skating is good in winter.

運動隨著季節而改變。人們在冬天和夏天玩不一樣的運動遊戲。在溫暖的天氣划船很有趣，然而在冬天滑雪就很棒。

People from different areas may not be able to understand each other, but after a game on the sports field, they often become good friends. Sports help to train a person's character. One learns to fight hard, to win without pride and to lose with grace.

不同地區的人們不一定彼此了解，但是在運動場上的一場比賽之後，他們常常會變成好朋友。運動有助於訓練一個人的個性，學習奮力拼博，勝不驕，敗不餒。

25. Sports help to keep people healthy and make them live <u>happily</u>.
運動有助於人們維持健康，活得<u>快樂</u>。

26. Sports change with the <u>seasons</u>.
運動隨著<u>季節</u>而改變。

27. Sailing is <u>fun</u> in warm weather.
在溫暖的天氣划船很<u>有趣</u>。

28. <u>Skating</u> is good in winter.
在冬天<u>滑雪</u>很棒。

29. People from different <u>areas</u> may not be able to understand each other, but after a game on the sports field, they often become good friends.
不同<u>地區</u>的人們不一定彼此了解，但是在運動場上的一場比賽之後，他們常常會變成好朋友。

30. One learns to fight hard, to win without pride and to <u>lose</u> with grace.
一個人學習奮力拼博，勝不驕和<u>敗</u>不餒。

全新英語聽力測驗試題
Final Test

I、Listen and choose the right picture.（根據你所聽到的內容,選出相應的圖片。）
（6分）

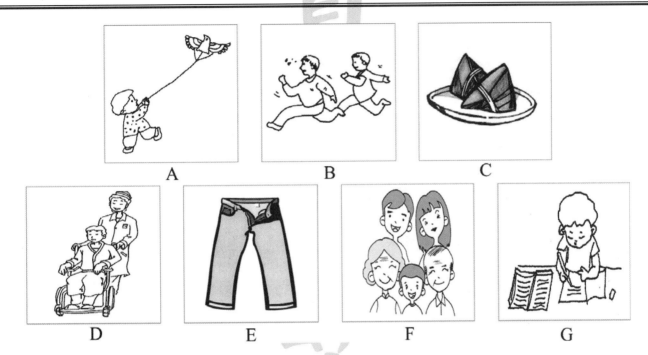

A   B   C

D   E   F   G

1. Mr. Li broke his left leg so he is in hospital now.
   （Li 先生摔斷了腿所以他現在在醫院。）
   答案：(D)

2. Yesterday, my mum bought a new pair of jeans for me as my birthday present.
   （昨天我媽買了一條牛仔褲給我當生日禮物。）
   答案：(E)

3. Running is good for your health. （跑步對你的健康有益。）
   答案：(B)

4. In autumn, it's fun to fly kites in the countryside. （秋天在鄉下放風箏很有趣。）
   答案：(A)

5. Look, this is my family photo. （看，這是我的家庭照。）
   答案：(F)

6. It's a tradition that people in China eat rice dumplings to celebrate the Dragon Boat Festival.（中國人吃粽子來慶祝端午節是一種傳統。）

答案：(C)

II、Listen and choose the best response to the sentence you hear.（根據你所聽到的句子,選出最恰當的應答句。）(6分)

7. How do you get on with your new deskmate?（你和你同桌的同學相處得如何？）
   (A)I'm fine.（我很好。）
   (B)We get on well with each other.（我們彼此相處得很好。）
   (C)He is clever.（他很聰明。）
   (D)Yes, we do.（是的，我們是。）

   答案：(B)

8. What is your sister like?（你姊姊長得怎麼樣？）
   (A)She is good.（她很好。）
   (B)She likes music.（她喜歡音樂。）
   (C)She is tall and slim.（她又高又瘦。）
   (D)She is reading books.（她在讀書。）

   答案：(C)

9. My parents haven't been to Australia before.（我爸媽以前沒去過澳洲。）
   (A)So have I.（我也去過。）　　　　(B)Neither haven't I.（我也去過。）
   (C)So haven't I.（我也沒去過。）　　(D)Neither have I.（我也沒去過。）

   答案：(D)

10. Shall we go shopping this Sunday?（這個星期天我們去購物好嗎？）
    (A)I don't think so.（我不這麼認為。）　(B)OK, let's.（好，我們去吧。）
    (C)That's all right.（沒關係。）　　　(D)That's right.（對。）

    答案：(B)

11. Have a great day!（祝你有個很棒的一天。）
    (A)Thank you.（謝謝你。）　　　　(B)I hope not.（我不希望。）
    (C)It's good.（那很好。）　　　　(D)Yes, I have.（是，我有。）

    答案：(A)

12. Dad, I have won the first prize in the English contest.
（爸，我英語競賽贏得第一名。）
(A)Really? Congratulations!（真的嗎？恭喜恭喜！）
(B)Thanks.（謝謝。）
(C)It's nothing.（那沒甚麼。）
(D)Don't say so.（別這麼說。）
答案：(A)

Ⅲ、Listen to the dialogue and choose the best answer to the question you hear.
（根據你所聽到的對話和問題,選出最恰當的答案。）（6分）

---

13. W: I'd like to have more books and children's magazines in our school library.
（W: 我希望我們學校圖書館裡有更多書與兒童雜誌。）
M: I'd like to have more interesting clubs in our school.
（M: 我希望我們學校有更多有趣的社團。）
Q: What changes would the girl like to see in their school?
（Q: 女孩想看到她們學校有甚麼改變？）
(A)More display boards.（更多展示板。）
(B)More interesting clubs.（更多有趣的社團。）
(C)More books and children's magazines in the library.
（圖書館裡有更多書與兒童雜誌。）
(D)Less homework.（少一點功課。）
答案：(C)

14. M: How much does the apple pie cost?（M: 蘋果派要多少錢？）
W: Three yuan each. If you want two, five yuan is OK.
（W: 一個三元。如果你買兩個，五元就好。）
Q: How much should the man pay if he wants to buy one apple pie?
（Q: 如果那個男人想買一個蘋果派，他應該付多少錢？）
(A)2.5 yuan.（二塊半。） (B)3 yuan.（三元。）
(C)5 yuan.（五元。） (D)3.5 yuan.（三塊半。）
答案：(B)

15. M: Which grade are you in, Mary?（M: Mary，妳幾年級？）

    W: I am in Grade 8. What about you, Frank?（W: 我八年級。Frank，你呢？）

    M: I am one year older than you.（M: 我比你大一歲。）

    Q: Which grade is Frank in?（Q: Frank 幾年級？）

    (A)In Grade 9.（九年級。）　　　　　(B)In Grade 8.（八年級。）

    (C)In Grade 7.（七年級。）　　　　　(D)In Grade 6.（六年級。）

    答案：(A)

16. M: How do you go to school, Linda?（M: Linda，妳怎麼上學？）

    W: I walk to school. It takes me about 10 minutes to get there. Do you go to school on foot, Fred?

    （W: 我走路上學。我到學校大概要花十分鐘。Fred，你走路上學嗎？）

    M: No, I go to school by underground, and then by bus.

    （M: 不是，我去學校要先搭地鐵再搭公車。）

    Q: Who lives closer to school, Linda or Fred?

    （Q: 誰住得離學校比較近，Linda 還是 Fred？）

    (A)Linda.　　　　　(B)Fred.　　　　　(C)Both.　　　　　(D)Neither.

    答案：(A)

17. W: What's the time by your watch, Jerry?（W: Jerry，你的手錶現在幾點？）

    M: Half past six. But my watch is five minutes fast.

    （M:六點半。但是我的錶快了五分鐘。）

    Q: What is the time now?（Q: 現在幾點？）

    (A)6:30.（六點三十分。）　　　　　(B)6:25.（六點二十五分。）

    (C)6:35.（六點三十五分。）　　　　　(D)6:20.（六點二十分。）

    答案：(B)

18. M: Can I help you, sir?（M: 先生，我能為你服務嗎？）

    W: I'd like to send these letters to Sydney and the parcel to Melbourne.

    （W: 我要寄這些信去雪梨，還要寄這個包裹去墨爾本。）

    M: Let me weigh them first.（M: 我先替它們秤重。）

    Q: Where does this dialogue probably take place?

    （Q: 這段對話大概發生在甚麼地方？）

    (A)At a restaurant.（在餐廳。）　　　　　(B)In an office.（在辦公室。）

    (C)At the post office.（在郵局。）　　　　　(D)At the police station.（在警察局。）

    答案：(C)

Listen to the dialogue and decide whether the following statements are True (T) or False (F). (判斷下列句子內容是否符合你所聽到的對話內容,符合的用"T"表示,不符合的用"F"表示。)（6分）

One day, an aeroplane left Los Angeles for London. Halfway across the Atlantic, the captain spoke to the passengers, "Good evening. This is your captain speaking. I'm afraid one of our engines has just stopped. But don't worry. We can fly on only three engines. But I'm afraid we'll arrive in London one hour late."

有一天，一架飛機從洛杉磯飛往倫敦。在橫越大西洋的半途中，機長對旅客說：「晚安。這是機長的談話。恐怕我們其中一個引擎已經停止運轉了。但是別擔心。我們可以靠另外三個引擎飛行。很遺憾我們會晚一個小時抵達倫敦。」

Half an hour later, the captain spoke to the passengers again, " Ladies and gentlemen, another engine has just stopped. But don't worry! We can fly on only two engines. But I'm afraid we'll arrive in London two hours late."

半小時後，機長又對乘客說話：「各位女士、各位先生，另一個引擎也在剛才停止了。但是別擔心！我們可以靠另外兩個引擎飛行。但恐怕我們會晚兩個小時抵達倫敦。」

Half an hour later, the captain spoke again. " Ladies and gentlemen, another engine has just stopped. But don't worry! We can fly on only one engine. But I'm afraid we'll arrive in London three hours late."

半小時後，機長又說了話：「各位女士、各位先生，另一個引擎也在剛才停止了。但是別擔心！我們可以靠另外一個引擎飛行。但恐怕我們會晚三個小時抵達倫敦。」

One passenger then said to another, " Oh,no! If that last engine stops, we'll stay in the sky all night!"

然後一位乘客對另一位乘客說：「喔，不！如果最後一個引擎也停止了，我們整個晚上就會待在天上了。」

19. The aeroplane was flying from London to Los Angeles. (飛機從倫敦飛往洛杉磯。)

    答案：(F 錯)

20. There are four engines on the plane. (飛機上有四個引擎。)

    答案：(T 對)

21. The aeroplane can't fly on only three engines. (飛機不能靠三個引擎飛行。)

    答案：(F 錯)

22. When the third engine stopped, one of the passengers went to see the captain.
（當第三個引擎停止時，一位乘客去看機長。）

答案：(F 錯)

23. If the last engine stopped, all the passengers would die.
（如果最後一個引擎停止，所有的乘客就會死亡。）

答案：(T 對)

24. In the end, the aeroplane arrived in London two hours late.
（最後，飛機慢了兩小時抵達倫敦。）

答案：(F 錯)

V、Listen and fill in the blanks.（根據你所聽到的內容,用適當的單詞完成下面的句子。每空格限填一詞。）（6分）

Germany is a modern country with a lot of traditions. Here are some examples. First, Germans like to shake hands when they are arriving or departing. It is a good way for a person to show that he or she is friendly. Second, a German who doesn't drink is not because he is shy or he is polite, but because he doesn't want to drink. Students can't drink in other countries, but please remember that the legal drinking age in Germany is 16. Next, take flowers if you are invited to a German's home. What's more, if you want to enter an office, you'd better knock at the door first. It's another way to show your politeness. Finally, if you want to have a birthday party, you should provide food and drinks for all the people.

德國是一個擁有許多傳統的現代化國家。這裡有許多例子。首先，德國人到達或離開的時候喜歡握手。這是一個表現他或她很友善的好方法。第二，一個德國人不喝酒不是因為他很害羞或是很有禮貌，而是因為他不想喝。其他國家的學生不能喝酒，但是請記住在德國合法的飲酒年齡是十六歲。其次，如果你受邀前往一個德國人的家，請帶著花。還有，如果你想進入一間辦公室，你最好先敲門。這是另一個表現禮貌的方法。最後，如果你想辦生日派對，你應該為所有人提供食物和飲料。

25. Shaking hands is a way to show a person is <u>friendly</u>.
握手是表現一個人<u>友善</u>的方法。

26. The legal drinking age in Germany is <u>16</u>.
在德國合法的飲酒年齡是<u>十六歲</u>。

27. Take <u>flowers</u> if you are invited to a German's home.
如果你受邀前往一個德國人的家，請帶著<u>花</u>。

28. Knock before you <u>enter</u> an office.
<u>進入</u>辦公室以前你要敲門。

29. <u>Provide</u> food and drinks for all the people if you have a <u>birthday</u> party.
如果你舉辦<u>生日</u>派對，你要<u>提供</u>食物和飲料。

全新英語聽力測驗【八年級/高階版上】

出版者：夏朵文理補習班

　　　　建如資訊股份有限公司

發行出版社：禾耘圖書文化有限公司

地址：新北市新店區安祥路 109 巷 15 號

電話：02-22007291　傳真：02-29426087

劃撥帳號：50231111 禾耘圖書文化有限公司

總經銷：紅螞蟻圖書有限公司

地址：台北市 114 內湖區舊宗路 2 段 121 巷 28 號 4 樓

網站：www.e-redant.com

電話：02-27953656　傳真：02-27954100

劃撥帳號：16046211 紅螞蟻圖書有限公司

ISBN 978-986-8858-42-8

本書由華東師範大學出版社有限公司授權夏朵文理補習班及
建如資訊股份有限公司出版發行。

定價 380 元